Fashion: Color, Line, and Design

Fashion: Color, Line, and Design

Second Edition

Leslie Ruth Peltz

Bobbs-Merrill Educational Publishing   Indianapolis

Copyright © 1980 by The Bobbs-Merrill Company, Inc.
Printed in the United States of America. All rights reserved. No
part of this book shall be reproduced or transmitted in any form
or by any means, electronic or mechanical, including photo-
copying, recording, or by any information or retrieval system,
without written permission from the Publisher:

    The Bobbs-Merrill Company, Inc.
    4300 West 62nd Street
    Indianapolis, Indiana 46268

Second Edition
Second Printing 1980
Interior and Cover Design by David Stahl

Library of Congress Cataloging in Publication Data

Peltz, Leslie Ruth.
    Fashion: color, line, and design.

    (Fashion merchandising series)
    Edition of 1971 published under title: Color, line, and
design.
    Includes bibliographical references.
    1. Fashion. I. Title.
TT518.P4   1980   746.9′2   79-25640
ISBN 0-672-97277-8

Contents

	Introduction	1
Chapter 1	Color	3
	Color Psychology and Symbolism	
	Color and Fashion	
	Color Terms	
	Color Theory	
	Color Schemes	
	Color Terms	
	Projects for Mixing Pigments	
	Other Color Projects	
Chapter 2	Clothing Details	17
	Ready-To-Wear Silhouettes	
	Dresses, Skirts, and Shirts	
	Coats, Jackets, and Suits	
	Pants	
	Necklines and Collars	
	Sleeves and Cuffs	
	Construction Details	
	Projects for Clothing Details	
	Bibliography	
Chapter 3	Outline of Costume History	45
	Egyptian	
	Babylonian-Assyrian	

Pre-Hellenic
Greek
Etruscan
Roman
Byzantine
Middle Ages
Renaissance
Seventeenth Century
Eighteenth Century
Nineteenth Century
Twentieth Century
Projects for Costume History
Bibliography

Chapter 4   National Costumes **77**
Europe
  England
  Scotland
  Denmark
  Norway
  Sweden
  Finland
  Lapland
  The Netherlands
  Germany
  Switzerland
  Austria
  France
  Spain
  Portugal
  Italy
  Greece
  Yugoslavia
  Bulgaria
  Albania
  Hungary
  Rumania
  Poland
  Soviet Union
  Turkey
The Middle East
Iran
Afghanistan
India and Pakistan
Southeast Asia

Contents　　　　　　　　　　　　　　　　　　　　　　　　　　　　　vii

People's Republic of China
Korea
Japan
Africa
United States of America
Mexico
Central and South America
Projects for National Costumes
Bibliography

Chapter 5　　　　　　　　　　Design Motifs 103
Straight and Curved Lines
Geometric Shapes
Shapes from Nature
Freeform or Nonrepresentational Shapes
Combinations of Motifs
Projects for Design Motifs
Bibliography

Chapter 6　　　　　　　　　　Fabric Design 115
A Successful Design
Repeat of the Design
Colors of the Design
History of Fabric Printing
Projects for Fabric Design
Bibliography

Chapter 7　　　　　　　　　　Fashion Drawing 127
Basic Figure Drawing
Drawing Clothing
Pose and Clothing Relationship
Pose and Customer Size/Image Relationship
Projects for Fashion Drawing
Bibliography

Bobbs-Merrill Educational Publishing
Fashion Merchandising Series

Executive Leadership
Fashion Accessories
Fashion Buying
Fashion: Color, Line, and Design
Fashion Direction and Coordination
Fashion Merchandising Internship Program Workbook
Fashion Textiles and Laboratory Workbook
 (with Fashion Textile Kit)
Fashion Vocabulary and Dictation
Fashion Writing
Home Furnishings
Merchandising Mathematics
Principles of Personal Selling
Selected Cases in Fashion Marketing (2 Volumes)

Introduction

The world of fashion is a world of change. In your fashion career, you will need an ability to recognize and predict trends, and this text will help you to do so. It will introduce you to the basics of color, silhouette, design, historical and ethnic costumes, and fashion drawing. This text is not intended to be a manual on how to design clothing, but rather a source book on the why of fashion, with an eye toward how to merchandise fashion.

Knowledge of color theory is very important in fashion merchandising. In clothing and accessories, the color of the material may be more influential than the styling details when it comes time to make the sale. It takes practice to develop the eye for color that is necessary for a buyer, coordinator, stylist, fashion writer, or colorist. You are probably aware that the physical and psychological effects of color on an individual determine color popularity. A knowledge of color mixing will help you to recognize the casts of a color, for example, green can have a bluish cast or brown can have a reddish cast. Knowledge of color mixing will also enable you to describe colors clearly for reports and articles. This text will teach you the basics of color theory.

In order to describe fashion items clearly and accurately, you must be familiar with styling terminology, and you must be able to recognize styling details in garments and accessories. This text will give you the terminology of styling details, silhouette, color, and material so that you can write fashion reports for stores, buying offices, magazines, newspapers, and manufacturers.

The design of a garment or accessory involves the combination of proportion, color, and silhouettes. Most of the silhouettes have a historical base. Over the centuries, styles have been adapted and readapted to correlate with the attitudes and events of the times. For example, the Victorian period (late 1800's) was a time of rigid adherence to Victoria's pompous moral conservatism. Corsets, padding, lacing, and metal and wooden stays were fashionable to support the body in a righteous stance. In a more relaxed period, such as the one of the Incroyables and the Merveilleuse (1790's), the clothing is cut looser, and the fabrics, shoes, and accessories contribute to a natural, comfortable look.

This text will also give you an overview of national costumes, another resource area for clothing designs. Rich and colorful costumes, such as the silk kimonos of the Japanese, the ornately embroidered blouses of the Hungarian and other European peasants, and the beaded tunics and moccasins of the American Indians, as well as simple costumes, such as the Mexican shirt and trousers, all serve as inspiration to today's designers. Knowledge of both historical and national dress will aid in your ability to identify and predict fashion trends.

Two chapters of the text deal with design. Design motifs for clothing and accessories are created from all kinds of lines and from shapes, which can be geometric, or inspired by nature, or freeform. This text will give you a repertoire of design motifs and will instruct you in how to repeat a motif and in the other factors involved in the creation of a successful fabric design.

It will be a great asset for you to be able to draw a well-proportioned fashion figure — not necessarily one that is a perfect illustration, just a well-proportioned figure. Fashion design begins with the figure. Traditionally the designs for each season emphasize a particular area of the female figure — the legs, the waistline, or the bosom, for example. The designs for the male figure usually follow in concept. Wherever the emphasis is placed, the proportion of the body stays fairly constant. This text will give you the opportunity to draw basic fashion figures.

In summary, you will have a knowledge of color (including an understanding of color theory), familiarity with styling terminology, awareness of fashion design history and national costumes, knowledge of design motifs and their applications, and a technique for drawing a well-proportioned fashion figure after studying this text. Each of these will contribute to your advancement in the fashion industry and to your fun in it.

1 Color

A store advertises a red sweater . . . do you think of tomatoes, strawberries, blood . . . a fire engine? Do certain colors make you happy and others made you sad? Do you have a favorite? The eye beholds color, but the mind *interprets* the sensations received. Everyone perceives color differently, feeling color as well as seeing color.

Color Psychology and Symbolism

Every person responds to color and has definite color preferences. Faber Birren has studied color extensively. His *Light, Color and Environment* and *Color Psychology and Color Theory* are good supplemental reading. Many studies of people and their responses to color have been done, and from these studies generalities begin to take form. The most-liked color is blue, followed by red, then by green, violet, orange, and yellow. Light colors are usually preferred over dark ones, as are primaries over intermediates, and pure hue over grayed hue. Introverts generally prefer neutral colors, while extroverts generally prefer bright colors. Neutral colors are considered to be more sophisticated. Cool colors are thought to be more comfortable in hot climates, and warm colors more comfortable in cold climates. Yet bright, hot colors are used in clothing designed for warm, sunny regions. Color awareness is greater today than ever before.

Studies of the psychological effect of color have been made. Researchers include Josephine Smith (color and infants), Kurt Goldstein (color and judgment), Heinz Werner (color and sound), Eric Mosse (color and paranoia), and Rorschach (color and epileptics). One study shows that babies react to bold, bright colors and show a preference for red.[1] Certain colors have been associated with specific forms of mental illnesses, particularly red with manic tendencies, green with psychosis, and blue with schizophrenia.[2] Blood pressure and respiratory rate can be increased under red light and decreased under blue light.[3]

Colors have symbolic meanings, evoking definite, individual reactions. To illustrate this, complete the Color Association Chart according to your own feelings, before reading any

---

[1] T. Berry Brazelton, "What Do Newborns Really See?," *Redbook's Young Mother* (1977): 28-29.

[2] Faber Birren, *Light, Color and Environment* (New York: Van Nostrand Reinhold Co., 1969), pp. 30-31.

[3] Ibid., p. 19.

further. Jot down whatever thought or image comes to your mind.

Favorite colors tend to reflect the personality. Red is positive, aggressive, exciting, and fits an outgoing, fiery-tempered person. Orange is exciting, and also glowing, but its tones and shades are preferred to its hue. Yellow is the most luminous color and is cheerful, but it is the least-liked color, sometimes being associated with sickness, cowardice, and introspection. Blue, the most popular color, is calming, peaceful, and makes you feel sensitive. Green is fresh and restful; it is the color of plants and the sea, but it is also associated

Color Association Chart. Complete the chart with as many descriptive words as possible.

YELLOW	RED	BLUE	ORANGE	VIOLET

GREEN	BLACK	WHITE	GRAY	BROWN

with jealousy. Blue-green is a flattering color to most people. Violet is cooling, but tends to be melancholy; it has been associated with older women. Purple is also soothing, though richer than violet; it signifies royalty and also mourning. White is airy, and sometimes cold; it implies innocence and, of course, is the traditional bridal color. Black can be fearful or formal; it can mean terror, death, or depression. In the twentieth century, black has come to be associated with sophistication. Gray is sedate and cold; it is a popular neutral. Brown is considered earthy, but is most liked by people with an educated, sophisticated eye.

Colors have varying connotations. A blue, green, or pale violet room is pleasantly restful. A red room is stimulating. Pale blue is associated with baby boys, and pink with baby girls. Pale yellow, mint green, and white are neutral. Vermilion, orange, yellow, and sea green are food colors. Aqua and soft green are watery. Fire engines are now often white or yellow for higher visibility. A red light means stop, and a green one, go; yellow-orange means caution.

Look at a flower garden and see how the reds, oranges, yellows, blues, violets, pinks, and whites of flowers, the green stems, leaves, and grass, the brown earth, tree trunks, and blue sky all harmonize beautifully. In nature there is no such thing as an unorthodox color combination. The fashion merchandiser with an eye toward nature knows that most colors work well together if the proper proportions are used.

Color and Fashion

Color is an important part of fashion apparel. The colors in an apparel line can be as significant as the silhouettes. Designers carefully choose their fabric colorations to make definite statements, sometimes using one color throughout a line and other times using a coloration for groups in a line. Colors combined for use in prints must harmonize either in a classical or an unorthodox way. Sometimes the unusual combination of one designer eventually becomes a standard for all designers.

Traditionally color has had seasonal associations. Dark and rich colors were designated for winter, while pale and pastel colors were designated for summer. Now that wardrobes have become less seasonal, the use of color is less restricted. White, beigy neutrals, and misty pastels appear in winter apparel collections. Bright, bold, hot colors are seen throughout the year. Navy, black, and brown are seen in both summer-weight fabrics and in winter wools.

Contemporary men's wear has generally been less changeable than women's wear, yet, today, color has clearly made significant inroads. Black, navy, gray, brown, and camel remain important colors for suits, slacks, and sport jackets, but other colors are appearing in the plaids, stripes, and patterns more men are now wearing. Other colors predominate in sportswear. Shirts, ties, sweaters, socks, and shoes must now color coordinate with the suit or slacks and sport jacket. Many men have a collection of shirts ranging from classic white to bold, multicolored prints. Today's fashion-conscious man also has a choice of bright colors in prints and solids for his underwear.

Another apparel area that has blossomed in color is the area of active sportswear for both men and women. Color in the tiniest bikini or in a slick tank suit livens up the pools and beaches all over the world. Tennis club members may still prefer traditional white on the courts, but color is also on the courts in trims and in coordinating jackets and accessories. Physical fitness used to bring to mind the image of runners wearing drab sweat suits. Now the image is of hills, trails, streets, and tracks inundated with clear, bright colors on the move. Ski slopes are vibrant with color, from patterned caps to boldly colored goggles and boots. See Figure 1-1 (Photo is courtesy of *Ski Magazine*).

Figure 1-1. Ski Wear in Clear, Bright Colors Inundates the Slopes.

Color

Fashion means coordination of color in accessories as well as in clothing. Cosmetic companies regularly introduce new colors to their product lines so that makeup will flatter the colors of the wardrobe. Eyeglass manufacturers have also taken color seriously, since many people have a wardrobe of frames to coordinate with their clothes. Color does not stop with the frame, but now goes on — tinted lenses are available for both indoor and outdoor wear.

Color is important in home furnishings. It can make a room look brighter, larger, or warmer. It sets the mood for the living environment. Colors of walls, windows, floors, and furniture must coordinate if the desired mood is to be set, and lighting must enhance the colors. The type or period of furniture chosen may influence the color schemes. If a person has a strong dislike for a particular color, he or she would do well not to choose that color for the home. Home surroundings should flatter the person who lives in them. There are trends in color for home furnishings just as there are trends in color for apparel. Accessories to home furnishings need to be included in color schemes just as accessories to apparel are.

Today a variety of color is available for the whole house, including towels in marvelous, bright colors and patterns and sheets, pillowcases, and comforters in delicate prints, bold patterns, and intense colors (see Figure 1-2). (White bed linens are almost extinct.) Placemats and napkins adorn tables in the latest fashion fabrics. Plastic dishes and utensils come in crayon colors. Kitchen appliances have long been available in color. Now available are items such as orange-colored coffee grinders, bright blue bowls, lemon yellow frying pans, red spatulas, green canisters, brown dish racks, and multicolored flowered cooking pots. The attractiveness of utilitarian design, which emphasizes the practical over the aesthetic, is heightened by the creative use of color.

Many people deal with color on a professional level. Fashion *designers* choose their own color schemes, then work with textile houses to obtain the proper fabrics. Mass-market apparel manufacturers often employ a *stylist,* who chooses the fabrics and colorations. Textile manufacturers, fiber producers, yarn producers, and leather companies all have *colorists*. Colorists foresee trends and choose the colors that will go into a company's products. Colorists for textile, fiber, and yarn producers generally work one year in advance of the season; colorists for leather houses work two years in advance. These textile, fiber, and yarn producers and leather houses make color swatch cards twice a year in the colors that colorists consider important for the future season. The colors of these swatch cards are well-researched and carefully developed. The colorist or stylist usually chooses a theme, and the colors are then named to fit that theme. The "peach" that a tricot fabric manufacturer is running can be totally different from the "peach" that a leather house is running. See how many names you can create for each color on the Color Name Chart.

It is costly and impractical for a producer to change all colors each season. Some colors are basic and are repeated successfully over many seasons: for example, white, black, navy, and beige. Other colors have a life of only a few seasons, for example, cranberry. A successful dark color in winter can be a successful accent color in spring and summer. Each season builds on the seasons before it.

Color is not simple. It is all around us in many forms. It permeates every part of life. Many people even dream in color. Do not be afraid to use color. Experiment with mixing pigments, with coordinating the colors in your wardrobe, with decorating your home in coordinating colors. Merchandise the products of your company more effectively through color awareness.

Figure 1-2. "Empress Garden" Design by Fieldcrest Is an Example of the Variety of Prints, Patterns, and Colors Available for Home Furnishings.

Color

Color Name Chart. Complete the chart with as many descriptive names for color as possible.

RED	PINK	YELLOW	ORANGE	GREEN

TURQUOISE	BLUE	VIOLET	BEIGE	BROWN

WHITE	BLACK	GRAY	SILVER	GOLD

Color Terms

A knowledge of basic color language will help you to discuss and understand color. A few basic terms will be defined before theories of color are discussed.

Pigment — dry coloring matter to be mixed with water, oil, or another base to produce paint, dye, or ink.

Primaries — the basic colors that are almost impossible to form by mixing other colors. In pigments, they are yellow, red, and blue (see the Color Wheel inside the front cover).

Secondaries — colors that are equal combinations of the primaries. In pigments, yellow and red equals *orange*, red and blue equals *violet*, and blue and yellow equals *green*. Orange, violet, and green are secondaries (see the Color Wheel).

Intermediates — colors that are combinations of a primary and a secondary. In pigments, yellow and orange equals *yellow-orange*, red and orange equals *red-orange*, red and violet equals *red-violet*, blue and violet equals *blue-violet*, blue and green equals *blue-green*, and yellow and green equals *yellow-green*. Yellow-orange, red-orange, red-violet, blue-violet, blue-green, and yellow-green are intermediates (see Color Wheel).

Hue — a pure color, including the primaries, secondaries, and intermediates. Any color that does not have white, black, or gray added to it.

Tint — a hue and white.

Shade — a hue and black.

Tone — a hue and gray (or a hue with black and white).

Value — the lightness or darkness of a color as determined by the amount of black or white added to it. A high value color has a great deal of white in it; a low value color has a great deal of black. Value is measured on a vertical chart beginning with the blackest shade on bottom, the purest hue generally in the middle, and the whitest tint on the top (see Value Chart inside back cover).

Chroma — the intensity of a color as determined by the amount of gray in it. A color of high chroma is almost pure; a color of low chroma has a great deal of gray in it. Chroma is measured on a horizontal scale, right to left, beginning with the purest hue and ending with the grayest tone of it. Chroma is also called saturation (see Chroma Chart inside back cover).

Chromatic Colors — colors with a hue in them. They can be altered by adding other hues, black, white, or gray.

Achromatic Colors — the colors black, white, and gray. They can be made darker or lighter only by adding more black, white, or gray.

Color Theory

In 1666 Sir Isaac Newton identified color in light. He used a glass prism to refract (break) a ray of light into violet, blue, green, yellow, orange, and red. The band of color formed in this way is called the spectrum. The colors of the spectrum have different *wavelengths*. To get a picture of "wavelength," imagine a rolling wave. The distance between the crests of two waves next to each other is the wavelength. Red has the longest wavelength, violet has the shortest, and the wavelengths of the other colors are in between. You can see the spectrum when the sun's rays are refracted by raindrops, and a rainbow is formed.

Newton recognized a relationship between spectrum red and spectrum violet. He formed the first color circle based on the red and violet relationship. The colors extending from red toward violet on his circle are orange, yellow, green, blue, and indigo.

Much study and theorizing have been done since Newton devised his circle of color, or color wheel. Theories about primary colors generally fall into three categories: 1) color in light, 2) color in vision, and 3) color in pigment.

The first theory, devised in 1790, falls into the category of color in light. The primaries are red, green, and blue-violet. In light, red and green equals yellow; green and blue-violet equals turquoise; red and blue-violet equals magenta. Light mixture is *additive,* meaning when the three primaries are mixed, they produce white light. Albert H. Munsell, American colorist famous at the beginning of the twentieth century, based his color wheel on this theory, although his principal hues were red, yellow, green, blue, and purple.

The second theory belongs in the category of color in vision and was established by a German physiologist, Ewald Hering, in 1874. In vision there are four primary hues — red, yellow, green, and blue. Vision mixture is *medial,* meaning when these primaries are mixed, they produce gray. Hering's theory was the basis for Wilhelm Ostwald's color wheel, established in the early twentieth century. Ostwald's primaries were red, yellow, sea green, and blue. Ostwald also set up a color triangle (see inside back cover). Using this triangle, you can see the changes that a hue goes through with the addition of black, white, and gray. A hue such as yellow, preferably a primary or secondary, is at one corner. Black and white each form a corner. Lines connect the three colors. Gray rests on the line halfway between black and white. A *shade* (of yellow) rests on the line halfway between yellow and black. A *tint* (of yellow) rests on the line halfway between yellow and white. A *tone* (of yellow) is in the center of the triangle, and three lines run through it, one between yellow and gray, one between the tint and black, and one between the shade and white (see Color Triangle inside back cover).

The third theory of primary colors is based on the combination of pigments (paints, dyes, or inks) and was devised by J. C. LeBlon in 1730. Red, yellow, and blue are the primaries. Pigment mixture is *subtractive,* meaning when the primaries are mixed, they produce black or dark brown.

Primary red, blue, and yellow have many variations, and thus color circles (also color triangles, stars, and solids), though based on the primaries red, blue, and yellow, have differed through the years. The traditional color circle, such as the one with this text, has a clear yellow, a crimson red, and a cobalt blue. The circle devised by Herbert E. Ives, which is commonly used for printing, has a clear yellow, a magenta red, and a turquoise blue.

Color Schemes

It is possible to make many colors by mixing the three primaries, but better variation and wider range of intensity are achieved when more colors are used. To mix a fairly complete palette, the following pigments are suggested: cadmium or spectrum yellow, vermilion or spectrum red, turquoise blue, ultra-marine blue, purple, black, and white.

In developing color schemes it is important to realize that color can produce varying effects. The goal is usually to have a harmonious combination of colors that is pleasing to the eye. The following are some general principles regarding combination of colors. All pure hues generally look good with the addition of white or black. A hue with its tints and white produces a soft effect, one which was often used by the Impressionists.[4] A hue with

---

[4]The Impressionists, a school of painters that developed in France in the 1870's, used unmixed colors and small brush strokes to create the effect of luminosity. Monet was an Impressionist.

its shades and black produces a rich effect, used by the Old Masters.[5] Tint, tone, and shade harmonies result in a shadowy effect. Gray works well with such harmonies. Tints look good with white, shades with black, and tones with gray. Tints of light intensity hues (yellow, orange) look best, and shades of dark intensity hues (blue, violet) look best. Tints, tones, and black, or shades, tones and white make other interesting combinations. Harmonious effects can also be produced by using a hue with one of its tints, shades, and tones, and white, black, and gray.

Texture can change the intensity of a color. Red satin will seem more intense than flannel in the same red. Effects of transparency, luster, luminosity, and iridescence can be produced, depending on how the color is used. An overlay of pigment can make something appear transparent. An area of color can appear lustrous if it is small and if the hue is pure and stands out in contrast to black. An area that is to appear luminous must also be small, be of strong chroma, and have overall light. Gray contrasts can create an impression of iridescence.

Color Terms

The following are more terms basic to the study of color.

Tertiaries — colors that are combinations of secondaries. They form softened versions of primaries, that is, primaries of low intensity. In pigments, orange and violet equals low tone of red, violet and green equals low tone of blue, green and orange equals low tone of yellow. These low intensity colors are tertiaries.

Warm Hues — hues on the color wheel that give a feeling of warmth: yellow, yellow-orange, orange, red-orange, red. Red-violet and yellow-green overlap on the cool side. Warm hues are good highlighters because they tend to stand out in combination with other hues.

Cool Hues — hues on the color wheel that give a feeling of coolness: violet, blue-violet, blue, blue-green, green. Cool hues make good background colors because they tend to recede when in combination with other hues.

Monochromatic — a color scheme based on one hue, or on combinations of the hue with its tints, tones, and shades.

Complementary — a color scheme made up of two hues that are opposite each other on the color wheel, for example, red and green (see Types of Color Schemes inside front cover). Complementary color schemes using primaries and secondaries are bolder than those using intermediates. A complementary color scheme sometimes includes the tints, shades, and tones of the two complements.

Split-Complementary — a color scheme made up of a hue and the two hues adjacent to its complement (see inside front cover).

Analogous — a color scheme made up of hues that are next to each other on the color wheel. In an analogous color scheme, the best effects are produced when the middle hue is a primary or secondary and the adjacent hues are intermediates, for example, yellow-orange, orange, red-orange. By varying the tints, shades, and tones of the hue, interesting color schemes can be made (see inside front cover).

Split-Analogous — a color scheme made up of hues that are adjacent to each other on the color wheel but that are one hue apart, for example, red, violet, and blue; yellow-green, blue-green, blue-violet (see inside front cover).

---

[5] "Old Masters" refers to the distinguished artists, such as Rembrandt, of the 16th, 17th, or early 18th century.

Triadic — a color scheme made up of three hues that are equally distant from each other on the color wheel, for example, yellow, red, and blue; red-orange, blue-violet, yellow-green. This scheme can be varied by using tints, shades, and tones of the three colors (see inside front cover).

Projects for Mixing Pigments

1. **Color Triangle** — choose a hue from the color wheel (preferably a primary or secondary). Paint a matching swatch, then make your own color triangle (see Color Triangle inside back cover).

2. **Value Chart** — choose a hue and paint a 2×1 inch swatch which will be placed at No. 5 position as you count vertically from the bottom (see Chroma/Value Chart inside back cover). Add black to the hue to create shades (swatches No. 4 to No. 1); add white to the hue to create tints (swatches No. 6 to No. 9).

3. **Chroma Chart** — choose a hue and paint four different tones of the hue. (A tone is a hue that is grayed by adding gray pigment, black and white, or the complement of the hue on the color wheel.) Present the chart horizontally, with the pure hue on the right-hand side (see Chroma/Value Chart inside back cover).

4. **Color Schemes** — on tracing paper draw an abstract design 6×6 inches. Trace the design onto white paper six times. Choose six hues and their tints, shades, and tones. Color one 6×6 inch design in each of the following color schemes: monochromatic, complementary, split-complementary, analogous, split-analogous, and triadic (see Types of Color Schemes inside front cover).

5. **Tertiaries** — paint a color swatch for each of the tertiaries.

6. **Brown Chart** — many different paint mixtures will result in brown, for example, orange and black. Paint five 2 × 2 inch swatches of brown. Label each swatch stating the pigments used.

7. **Original Color Circle** — paint 12 color swatches 2 × 2 inches in the primaries, secondaries, and intermediates that will go through the primary family groups (yellow/orange/red/ violet/blue/green). Before you paste down the swatches to form the circle, cut them into an interesting shape to make the circle more unusual.

Other Color Projects

1. **Oral Presentation** — research color symbolism in one of the following areas and prepare a five-minute oral presentation.

   A. Flags and pennants
   B. Gems
   C. Signs of the Zodiac
   D. Amulets and talismans
   E. Flowers and plants
   F. Color names

2. **Swatch Card** — design and construct a swatch card for the incoming fashion season, to be used by any of the following: manufacturer, pattern company, magazine, coordinator, or consumer. The swatch card should include:

   A. An original theme
   B. Color samples, using fabric, yarn, beads, or paint
   C. Color names
   D. A written description of color and fabric trends for the season

Bibliography

Birren, Faber. ***A Grammar of Color.*** New York: Van Nostrand Reinhold Co., 1969.

Birren, Faber. ***Color in Your World.*** New York: Macmillan Co., 1966.

Birren, Faber. ***Color Psychology and Color Therapy.*** New Hyde Park, New York: Citadel Press, 1978.

Birren, Faber. ***Creative Color.*** New York: Van Nostrand Reinhold Co., 1961.

Birren, Faber. ***Light, Color and Environment.*** New York: Van Nostrand Reinhold Co., 1969.

Birren, Faber. ***Principles of Color.*** New York: Van Nostrand Reinhold Co., 1969.

Birren, Faber. ***Selling Color to People.*** New York: Van Nostrand Reinhold Co., 1956.

Birren, Faber, ed. ***The Color Primer: A Basic Treatise on the Color System of Wilhelm Ostwald.*** New York: Van Nostrand Reinhold Co., 1969.

Brazelton, T. Berry. "What Do Newborns Really See?" ***Redbook's Young Mother.*** (1977): 28-29.

Fabri, Ralph. ***Color: A Complete Guide for Artists.*** New York: Watson-Guptill, 1967.

Halse, Albert O. ***The Use of Colors In Interiors.*** New York: McGraw-Hill Book Co., 1968.

Sargent, Walter. ***The Enjoyment and Use of Color.*** New York: Dover Publications, Inc., 1964.

Taylor, F. A. ***Colour Technology.*** London: Oxford University Press, 1962.

2 Clothing Details

Clothing styles change from season to season, yet the basic elements of a garment remain the same. A designer's utilization of these basic elements with color and fabric is what makes the diversity of clothing styles.

The descriptions of clothing and construction details in this chapter are standard. You will not see all of these details used every season, but they are recurring, that is, a collar, sleeve, coat, or skirt not seen one year may be the most outstanding look the following year. It is important to know these clothing details and be able to recognize them in order to better understand and interpret fashion cycles and also fashion silhouettes.

Ready-To-Wear Silhouettes

Dresses, Skirts, and Shirts

A-Line — a dress or skirt that skims the waistline and flares to the hem. See Figure 2-3.

Asymmetric — a dress or skirt with an off-center or side closing.

Basque — a knitted shirt similar to a polo shirt but with horizontal stripes of contrasting colors, short sleeves, and a crew neck.

Bell — a skirt that curves from the hip toward the hem into a bell shape.

Bias — a dress made from cloth cut on the bias (see "Construction Details"). This figure-hugging silhouette was made famous by Mme. Vionnet, a French designer.

Blouson (BLUE-sun) — a dress or blouse silhouette with a loose top gathered into a waistline that appears dropped. The effect, even in a dress, is that of an overblouse. See Figure 2-1.

Body Shirt — a style used for both men's and women's shirts, having curved seams that make the shirt hug the body. It has no pockets, a long-pointed collar, and (usually) long sleeves. See Figure 2-5.

Bouffant or Ballet — a dress with a full skirt and a tight waistband. The bouffant is the traditional ballet dancer's costume and is also a basic style for children's wear. See Figure 2-1.

Chemise — a straight dress silhouette lacking a waistline (sometimes called a "sack"). A loose, short slip worn as a woman's undergarment is also a chemise. "Chemise" is the French word for shirt. In 1957 Spanish designer Balenciaga introduced the chemise. See Figure 2-1.

Circular — a skirt that forms a circle when laid flat. It is smooth across the hips and full below.

Corselet — a dress with a tight-fitting midriff that often has lacing through eyelets.

Dirndl (DURN-dil) — a dress with a close-fitting bodice, a low round or square neckline, and a full skirt gathered at the waist. It originated from the gaily printed, cotton native dress of Tyrol, a province of Austria. Today a dirndl dress or skirt often has curved side seams that eliminate some of the fullness at the hips. See Figure 2-3.

Draped — inspired by the costumes of ancient Greece, the term refers to a dress, skirt, or blouse that has fabric falling in soft folds. Parts of a garment are usually draped, such as a neckline or sleeve, rather than the entire garment. This look was made famous by Mme. Grés, a French designer.

Dress Shirt — a short- or long-sleeve man's shirt with a collar. It is generally in a solid color but can be striped, checked, or patterned.

Empire (am-PEER) — a dress with the waistline placed under the bust. This was the style favored by the Empress Josephine during the French Empire period of 1804 to 1814. Originally an empire dress had a high waist, deep

Figure 2-1. Dress Styles.

Blouson *Bouffant* *Chemise*

Clothing Details

neckline, short sleeves, and a long, straight skirt. See Figure 2-2.

Evening Shirt — a man's shirt for formal attire, having long sleeves, a wing collar, and a starched front. A man's evening shirt for semiformal attire has long sleeves, a pleated or ruffled front, and a spread collar (see "Necklines and Collars").

Flounce — a skirt which has one or more wide, decorative ruffles.

Godet (go-DAY) — a skirt with triangular inserts near the hem to add flare. See Figure 2-3.

Gored — a skirt or dress with shaped panels that add fullness to the garment. See Figure 2-3.

Jumper — a sleeveless dress without a collar that is meant to be worn over a blouse or sweater.

Kilt — a short, pleated skirt adapted from the costume of the Scottish Highlanders.

Kimono (ka-MO-na) — the native dress of Japan, worn by both men and women. It has short, wide sleeves that are cut with the back and front of the kimono from one piece of cloth. An obi, or wide sash, circles the waist and holds the garment together. This style is often used in loungewear. See Figure 2-2.

Man-Tailored — a woman's shirt styled after a man's, usually having a short-pointed collar, a buttoned-front closing, and long sleeves with a French or button cuff (see "Sleeves and Cuffs").

Maxi — a skirt, dress, or coat that stops at

Figure 2-2. Dress Styles.

Empire *Kimono* *Moyenage*

Figure 2-3. Skirt Styles.

A-Line

Godet

Gored Skirt

Dirndl

Sarong

Tiered Skirt

Clothing Details

or near the ankle. It was introduced during the 1967-1968 season.

Middy — a blouse adapted from the sailor's costume, having a low waist and long sleeves with a tight cuff. It has a collar, often in contrasting color (see "Sailor Collar").

Midi — a skirt, dress, or coat that stops at mid-calf. It was first introduced in 1967 by American designer Bill Blass.

Mini — a very short skirt or dress (four inches or more above the knee), introduced by English designer Mary Quant in 1967.

Monastic — a dress adapted from the heavy robe worn by a monk. It may have a hood, the front is bias cut, and there is usually a cord belt at the waistline.

Moyenage (mwa-yah-NAZH) — a dress with tight sleeves, a low, snug waist, and a full skirt. See Figure 2-2.

Peplum — a flared, hip-length tier attached at the waistline of a dress, coat, jacket, or blouse. See Figure 2-4.

Petal — a skirt with overlapping petals of fabric.

Pinafore — a sleeveless apronlike garment that can be worn alone or over other apparel. It often has ruffles at the shoulder. The pinafore was originally designed as a cover-up for children's clothing, but it is also used in women's apparel.

Pleated — skirts, dresses, or blouses, with folds of fabric pressed or stitched in place (see "Construction Details").

Polo Shirt — a short-sleeve knit shirt with a crew neck (see "Necklines and Collars"), with rib trim on the neckline and sleeve in a contrasting color. Originally the polo shirt was for men's and children's wear, but now it is also for women's wear. See Figure 2-5.

Princess — a close-fitting dress or coat that is gored (see "Construction Details") and has a full skirt. There is no break at the waistline. See Figure 2-4.

Sari — native costume of Hindu women. It is a long, rectangular piece of fabric that is wrapped around the body and can also cover the head.

Sarong — a skirt adapted from the native dress of the Malay Archipelago (a group of islands including the Philippines). It is a long piece of fabric that wraps around the lower part of the body and ties at the waist. See Figure 2-3.

Sheath — a straight slim-fitting skirt or dress that has no fullness and usually no belt. See Figure 2-4.

Shift — a loose dress without a waistline. It can be straight like a chemise or follow an A-line.

Shirtdress or Shirtwaist — a dress adapted from a man's shirt. It has a front closing that can stop at the waist, (usually) has a belt, and can be straight, flared, pleated, or gored. It can have short, long, or no sleeves, and can have a collar or be collarless. See Figure 2-4.

Skating — a short skirt extending only to the upper thigh, originally worn with a sweater for ice skating. It is usually circular but can also be pleated or gored.

Smock — a loose shirt or jacket with front and back yokes, patch pockets, cuffed sleeves, and a collar. It is traditionally a peasant shirt with smocking detail (see "Construction Details") on the yoke and cuffs. A smock is also used as a cover-up to protect clothing.

Sport Shirt — a man's short- or long-sleeve shirt worn with sporty attire. It can be brightly colored or patterned, or made in a novelty fabric.

Straight — a slim straight-line skirt that may have a few pleats at the hemline for ease in moving.

Tank Top — an unfitted, sleeveless top with a deep U-Neck. It can be worn alone or over a shirt or sweater.

22 Fashion: Color, Line, and Design

Figure 2-4. Dress Styles.

Peplum

Princess

Sheath

Shirtwaist

Trapeze

Trumpet

Clothing Details

Tiered—a skirt with layers of flounces. See Figure 2-3.

Trapeze—an exaggerated A-line style dress or coat first introduced by French designer Christian Dior in 1955. Yves St. Laurent popularized the trapeze in his 1958 collection for the House of Dior. The trapeze is also called the "tent" and has been widely used in maternity clothes. See Figure 2-4.

Trumpet—a skirt with pleats or godets (see "Construction Details") placed near the hem to form a flare like that of a trumpet.

T-Shirt—a plain, short-sleeve shirt with a crew or V-neck (see "Collars and Necklines"), usually in one color. It is also worn as underwear by men and boys.

Tunic—a blouselike garment, usually with short or long sleeves. It extends to mid-thigh, can have a belt, and is often worn over a skirt or pants. A sleeveless tunic with slit sides can be worn over a dress or pants.

Western Shirt—a man's or a woman's tapered shirt with yoke front and back, a pointed collar, two patch pockets with flaps, and fancy snap closures on front placket and cuffs. See Figure 2-5.

Wrap-Around—a dress, skirt, or coat that wraps around the body. It fastens with snaps or a hidden closure rather than with buttons or a zipper, and there is usually a belt to hold it in place.

Coats, Jackets, and Suits

Balmacaan (BAL-ma-can)—a loose-fitting topcoat with raglan sleeves and slash pockets. It is usually of wool tweed or is homespun, and often has water-repellent fabric on one side to make it reversible. See Figure 2-7.

Basque (BASK)—a woman's coat, jacket, or dress that has a tight, fitted bodice, adapted from a fisherman's jersey of the late nineteenth century.

Baseball Jacket—a short, snap-front jacket with knitted neck, cuffs, and bottom, and with slash pockets. Fashion baseball jackets are adapted from those worn by major league baseball teams,

Figure 2-5. Shirt Styles.

Body Shirt   *Polo Shirt*   *Western Shirt*

which were originally in two-toned fabric and embroidered with the team and player's name.

Battle Jacket — a jacket adapted from those worn by men in the United States Armed Forces during World War II. It is single-breasted, banded at the waist, and has patch pockets with flaps. It is also known as "Eisenhower jacket." See Figure 2-6.

Beachcoat — a man's or a woman's coat or jacket, usually made of an absorbent fabric, intended to be worn over bathing suits.

Bi-swing — a jacket often used for active sportswear. It has inverted pleats in back from the shoulder and a half-belted waist.

Blade Jacket — a jacket for men that has extra fullness across the shoulder

Figure 2-6. Jacket Styles.

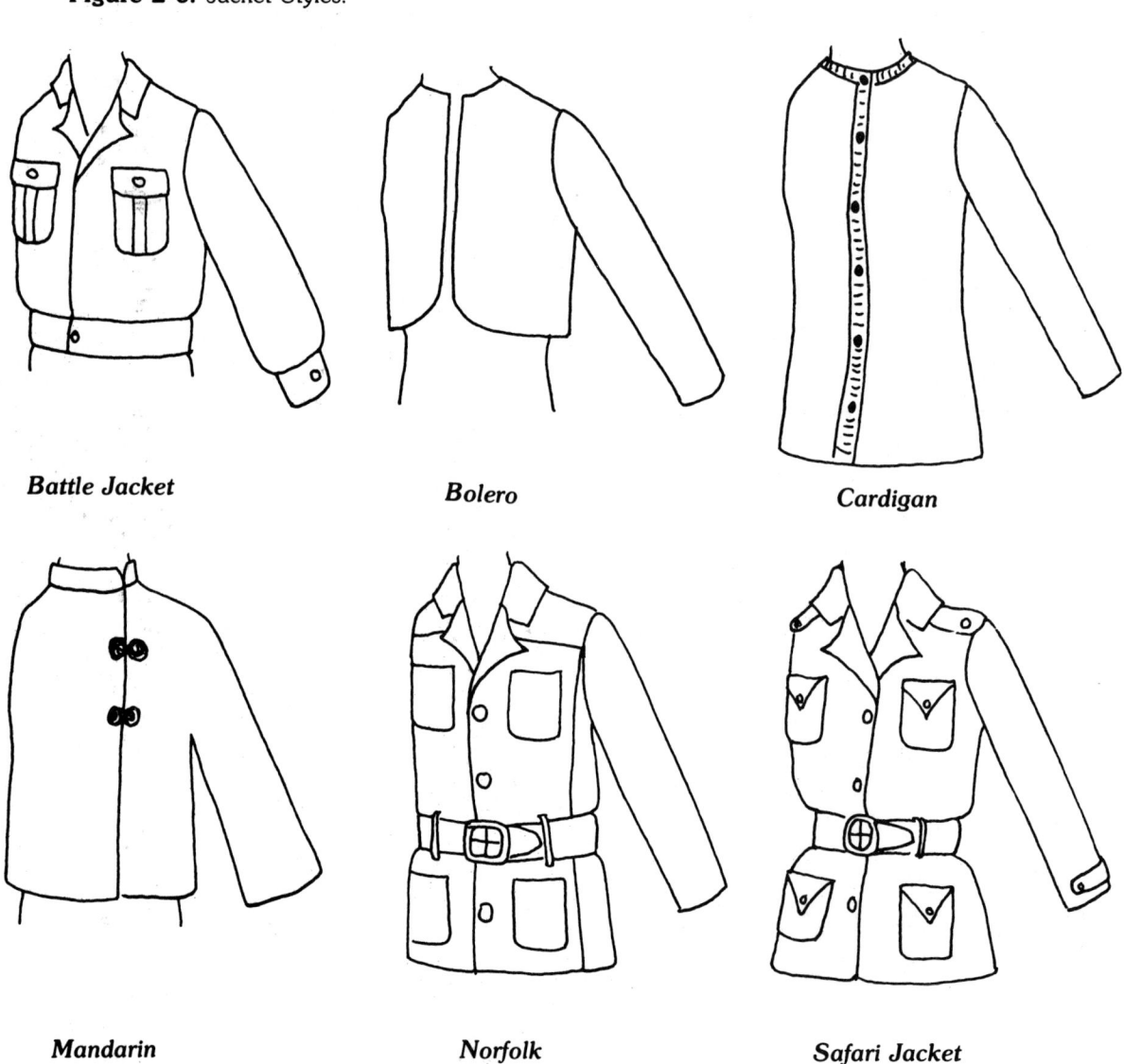

Battle Jacket

Bolero

Cardigan

Mandarin

Norfolk

Safari Jacket

Clothing Details

blades to give a broad appearance to the wearer.

Blazer — a sport jacket for men and women. It may be single- or double-breasted, solid-color or striped, or adorned with metal buttons and patch pockets.

Bloused — a woman's coat with a full bodice gathered into the waistband, usually having a slim skirt.

Bolero — a short, above-the-waist jacket adapted from a native Spanish costume. The bolero is open in front with a curved bottom hem, with or without sleeves. See Figure 2-6.

Box — a straight, loose-fitting beltless, single- or double-breasted coat with a fly front for men and women.

Burnoose — a loose, light-colored cloak with a hood.

Cape — a sleeveless outer garment that closes at the neck and hangs over the back and shoulders. It is often hooded or attached to a coat or dress, and can be any length or fabric.

Cardigan — a sweater, dress, jacket, or coat for men, women, or children, that is collarless and buttons down the front. It can have either a round or V-neck and is usually banded around the neck and down the front. See Figure 2-6.

Carrick — a fitted coat with three capes, each decreasing in size, adapted from the men's Victorian coat. See Figure 2-7.

Chesterfield — a semifitted coat, single- or double-breasted, beltless, with flap pockets, fly front, and a velvet collar. The chesterfield was originally for men, but is worn by women also. See Figure 2-7.

Continental Suit — a man's single-breasted, two-button jacket and trousers. The jacket has some shaping, side vents, narrow lapels, and a rounded front (see "Pants").

Conservative Suit — a man's single- or double-breasted jacket and trousers. The jacket has light padding in the narrow shoulders, short and narrow lapels, and a center vent (see "Pants").

Cutaway — a man's formal daytime coat, cut with a curve from the front waistline to the back tails.

Directoire (DEE-rek-twar) — coat for men and women inspired by the costumes from the French Directoire period, 1795 to 1799. It is fitted through the waist and has a flared skirt and a high, standing collar with lapels.

Dolman — a full coat with a dolman sleeve (see "Sleeves").

Duffle or Duffel — a boxy, knee-length sport coat of coarse, sturdy fabric, popularized in America as the "Loden" coat. It is unlined and closed with wooden toggles and hemp loops.

Edwardian Suit — an English-inspired man's single- or double-breasted jacket with four-button (or more) closing. It has a suppressed waist, deep center or side vents, and wide notched lapels. Trousers can be straight or flared.

English Drape — a single- or double-breasted man's or woman's jacket with extra fullness across the chest and shoulders, a fitted waist, and slim sleeves.

Eton Jacket — a short jacket very similar to a bolero that closes in the front and has a small, round, stiff white collar. It is adapted from the jacket worn by the boys at Eton, the famous English school.

Fencer's Jacket — a jacket adapted from the protective jacket worn by fencers. It is close-fitting, waist length, closed on the side or back, and has a high neckline.

Greatcoat — an English term for a heavy overcoat that sometimes has a belt, is usually double-breasted, and has a collar with a neck closing.

Inverness (in-ver-NESS) — an overcoat with a removable sleeveless cape. Inverness also refers to a long, sleeveless

Figure 2-7. Coat Styles.

Balmacaan

Carrick

Chesterfield

Polo Coat

Reefer

Trench Coat

Clothing Details

cape that is fastened at the neck. It is usually in plaid fabric.

Ivy League Suit — man's single-breasted, three-button, natural-shoulder (unpadded), unshaped jacket with narrow lapels and center vent, and trousers. A vest can be included.

Mackinaw or Lumberjacket — a short, heavy, double-breasted coat usually made in plaid wool.

Mandarin — a coat or jacket adapted from the costume of Chinese mandarins (high officials) during the Chinese Empire. It has a small stand-up collar, kimono sleeves, side slashes, and an asymmetric closing. See Figure 2-6.

Norfolk — a single-breasted, hip-length, belted jacket with patch pockets and yoke, and box pleats in the front and back. It is worn by both men and women. See Figure 2-6.

Officer's Coat or Guard's Coat — a coat similar to the coat worn by officers of the United States Armed Forces and by English guardsmen. It is double-breasted, with a broad collar, half belt, slash pockets, and an inverted back pleat.

Overcoat — a warm, heavy coat worn over other clothing.

Pants Coat — a women's casual coat, usually fingertip length, originally intended to be worn over pants. It can be made in a variety of styles and is also known as "car coat."

Pants Suit — a woman's suit consisting of a jacket or coat and a coordinating pair of pants.

Parka — a hooded jacket, often with a pile or fleece lining, used for active sports. The original parka was fur and came from the Eskimos.

Pea Jacket — a short single- or double-breasted coat of heavy woolen fabric such as melton cloth, worn by sailors for warmth. It has also been adapted for street wear as a winter coat.

Polo Coat — a boxy, single- or double-breasted coat with patch pockets, large buttons, welt seams, and a half or full belt. Originally it was made of natural-color camel's hair, but is now in other fabrics and colors.

Poncho — a rectangular piece of cloth with no seams and having a hole in the center for the head, adapted from the poncho worn by South American natives. It is made in many fabrics, including waterproof materials for rainwear.

Raincoat — a water-repellent or waterproof coat worn over clothing for protection from the rain. Many raincoats are highly styled and are worn as regular or all-weather coats.

Redingote — a French term for adaptations of the English riding coat. It is a simple coat, usually fitted and beltless, and worn with a coordinating dress.

Reefer — a single- or double-breasted woman's coat that is princess styled. See Figure 2-7.

Riding Coat — a long, single-breasted jacket with slanting pockets. The skirt is flared and has a center vent or two side vents in the back for comfort when the wearer is astride a horse. It is also known as "hacking jacket."

Safari Jacket — a jacket generally of a lightweight fabric, with lapels, four pockets, epaulets, and a belt, adapted from the jacket sportsmen wear on safaris. See Figure 2-6.

Shawl — a wrap originally worn by peasant women. It is a square piece of fabric folded on the diagonal to form a triangle, and is often fringed.

Shell — a separate warm lining that can be zipped, buttoned, or snapped into a coat.

Slicker — a loose, waterproof coat adapted from the fisherman's coat, originally made from an oil-treated fabric. It is more commonly made of vinyl today.

Ski Jacket — a lightweight but warm jacket designed for skiers. It is often made of water-repellent nylon to resist winds and moisture, is interlined with polyester fiber for warmth, and has a zipper front and a hidden hood.

Smoking Jacket — a man's lounging jacket intended to be worn at home over a shirt and trousers. It usually has a shawl collar and tie belt. In the 1960's French designer Yves St. Laurent adapted the look for women's evening clothes and called it "Le Smoking." He repeated the look over many seasons, into the 1970's, by changing the style somewhat with each collection.

Spencer — a short jacket that was the predecessor of the man's suit jacket. It is cut close to the body and has slim sleeves.

Sport Coat — a man's or woman's coat, often patterned, worn as a topcoat over casual attire.

Sport Jacket — a man's jacket, often checked, striped, or plaid, worn over contrasting or coordinating trousers.

Storm Coat — a warm outer coat worn by men, women, or children in cold weather. Usually it is double-breasted and belted and has a warm, detachable lining.

Stole — a long, scarflike piece of cloth or fur worn by women in place of a coat.

Suit — for men, a garment consisting of a jacket, trousers, and sometimes a vest. For women, a suit combines a jacket with a skirt and/or pants (and sometimes a vest). Each part is usually made from the same fabric.

Swagger — a coat with a full back, falling from the shoulders, having no belt. It has a detachable lining and a fur collar.

Tailleur (tay-YUR) — a woman's slim, single-breasted, well-tailored dress suit.

Tail Coat — a man's formal coat that has long tails in the back.

Topcoat — a lightweight overcoat worn by men and women.

Topper — a short topcoat also called "shortie," worn by women over a dress or suit.

Trench Coat — adapted from the World War I English Officers' coat, it is used now by men and women as a raincoat or sportcoat. It is double-breasted, with a wide belt, military collar, pockets, and shoulder flaps. See Figure 2-7.

Tunic — a short, tight-fitting jacket, often part of a uniform.

Tuxedo or Dinner Jacket — a man's semiformal single- or double-breasted evening jacket with a peaked or shawl collar. The tuxedo usually has matching trousers; the dinner jacket, contrasting trousers.

Ulster — a man's heavy, loose, double-breasted overcoat with a convertible collar and half or full belt.

Vest or Weskit — a garment for men, women, and children, either woven or knitted, which can be worn with pants or a skirt or coordinated as part of a suit. It is generally short, stopping at the waist or hips, and sleeveless. It can be V-neck, buttoned-front, pullover, or buttonless.

Windbreaker — a sport jacket with front zipper and elasticized waistband and cuffs. It is usually made of poplin or nylon and has a water-repellent finish. (When made of nylon, a windbreaker is called a "shell.") The windbreaker is worn by men, women, and children.

Wrap-Around — (see "Dresses").

Pants

Bell-bottom Pants — men's and women's pants that are narrow through the hips, then form a wide flare from the knee down. They can be cuffed and can have wide belt loops and pockets. See Figure 2-8.

Clothing Details

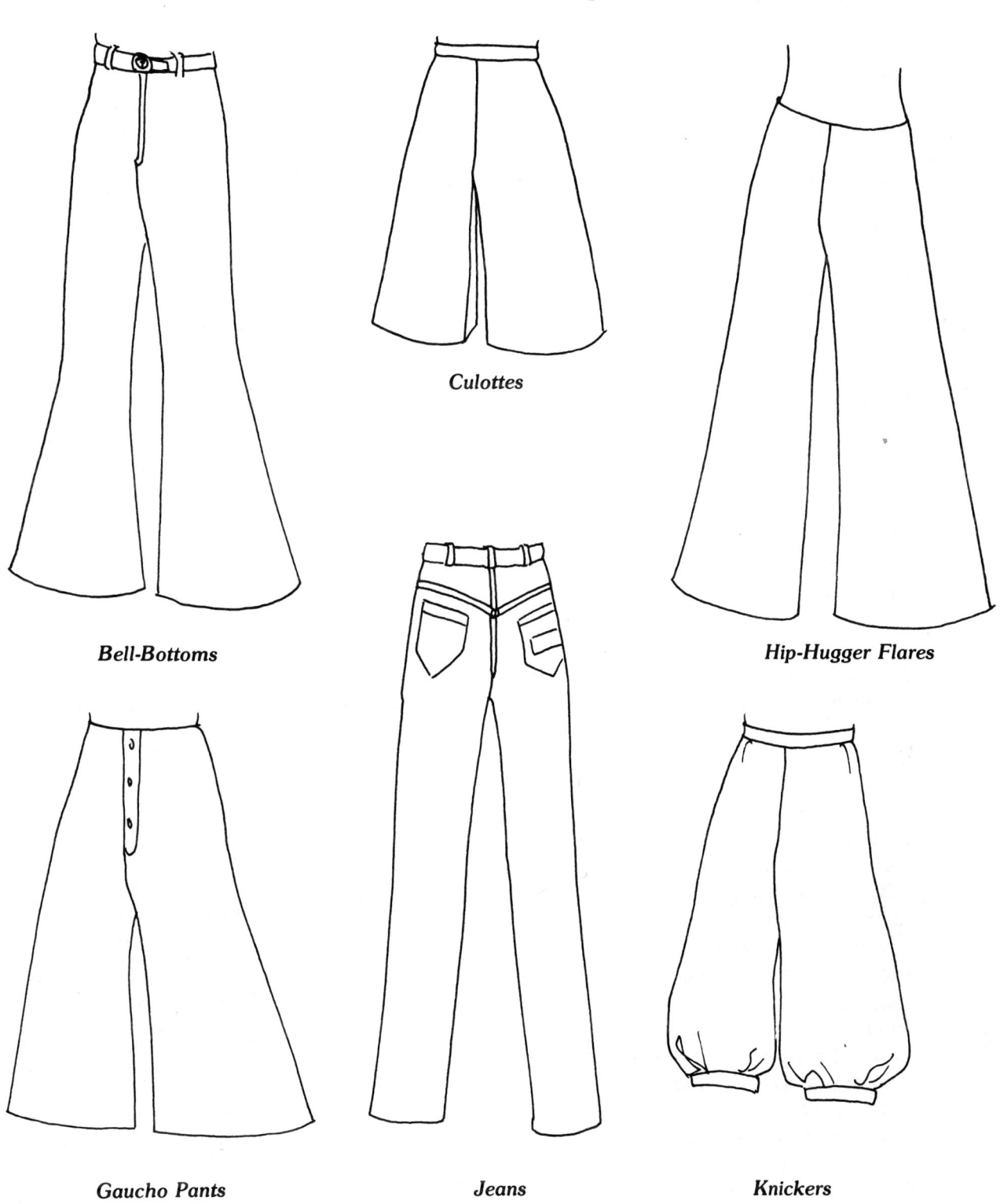

Figure 2-8. Pants Styles.

Culottes

Bell-Bottoms

Hip-Hugger Flares

Gaucho Pants

Jeans

Knickers

Continental Trouser — a man's trouser with an extended waistband, no belt loops, side adjustments, western or side-slashed pockets, and moderate- or narrow-tapered leg.

Conventional or Conservative Trouser — a man's pleated or unpleated trouser with either extended waistband or belt loops, side-slashed pockets, full- to moderate-tapered leg, and with cuffs or cuffless.

Culottes — women's short pants that look like a skirt, often with concealing front pleats, originally intended for golfing. See Figure 2-8

Dungarees — sturdy work pants for men, women, and children with curved front pockets, front zipper, and reinforcements at stress points. They are generally made in heavy-duty dungaree twill fabric.

Flared — men's or women's pants with legs that flare moderately or fully from the hip. See Figure 2-8.

Gaucho Pants — pants inspired by those of the South American cowboys. The pants have fitted hips, then flare into the middle of the calf where they stop. A version with a narrower flare is called "boot pants." See Figure 2-8.

Harem Pants — soft, full pants that are gathered above the ankle. They are often used for lounge wear or evening apparel.

Hip-hugger Pants — men's and women's pants that sit on the hipbone rather than on the waist. The rise, or distance between the waist and crotch, is short. The legs can be straight or flared. See Figure 2-8.

Ivy League — men's trousers with belt loops, side-slashed pockets, full- to moderate-tapered legs, and cuffs.

Jeans — men's, women's, and children's pants with yokes (western styling), front zipper, pockets in the yoke, and straight or flare leg. They were originally made in cotton jean cloth, but now are made in many fabrics. See Figure 2-8.

Jodhpurs (JOD-perz) — men's and women's riding pants that are full and loose from hip to calf, tight-fitting from calf to ankle.

Jumpsuit — a one-piece garment with or without sleeves, having straight or flare legs, that is an updated version of the industrial coverall. It is made in many styles and fabrics for men and women.

Knickers — shortened form of the term "knickerbockers." Knickers are loose pants for men and women that are gathered below the knee into a snug band. They are also called "plus fours." See Figure 2-8.

Overalls — loose pants with a panel that extends over the chest and is held in place by shoulder straps. Overalls originally were made in sturdy fabrics and worn by farmers or railroad men. Later they were adapted for children's wear, and now they are also worn as sportswear.

Pedal Pushers — slim pants that end just below the knee. "Toreador pants" are a tighter version and "clam diggers" a looser version.

Shorts — pants for men, women, and children that end anywhere from the top of the knee (Bermuda, or walking shorts) to the top of the thigh (short shorts).

Ski Pants — stretch pants designed for skiers. They may be loose or tight and usually have foot straps to hold them in place under ski boots.

Straight Pants — men's and women's pants that form a straight line from the hip to the ankle. They can have cuffs.

Trouser — (see Continental and Conventional Trousers).

Trumpet Pants — men's and women's pants that are slim to the calf where they flare into a bell.

Clothing Details

Necklines and Collars

Ascot — a scarf or tie originally worn at the racetrack in Ascot, England, tied with the wide ends hanging over each other and often held in place by a stickpin.

Backless — a neckline with a high front and no back.

Bateau (bah-TOW) — French for "boat." A bateau neckline is a wide neckline close to the neck that curves slightly from points on the shoulder seams. See Figure 2-9.

Bermuda — a small, round collar that has a straight edge extending from the center front to the rounded outer edge.

Bertha — a woman's capelike collar that extends from the neckline to over the shoulders. See Figure 2-9.

Bib — originally a tiny apron tied around the neck of an infant. It has been adapted to women's dresses and blouses.

Bow — a separate scarf or strip of fabric attached at the neckline, tied into a bow. It is also a man's tie looped into a bow.

Figure 2-9. Neckline and Collar Styles.

Bateau

Bertha

Button-Down Collar

Cowl

Halter

Buster Brown — a high, small, round collar, usually with a contrasting ribbon bow.
Button-Down — a collar with buttonholes on the points. The points button onto the shirt front. This collar is used on both men's and women's shirts. See Figure 2-9.
Camisole — a neckline adapted from the women's camisole slip, that is cut straight above the bustline and held by thin shoulder straps.
Cape — a small cape used as a collar.
Cardigan — (see "Coats").
Chinese — a small, stand-up collar slit in the front. It is also called mandarin, Nehru, or Mao and was originally part of Chinese native dress.
Choir Boy — a large collar with points adapted from those that choir boys wear. There is a big, self-tied bow under the collar.
Choker — a ribbon, piece of jewelry, scarf, or collar worn tight around the neck.
Chou (SHOO) — French for "cabbage." A chou is a ribbon or fabric-draped knot resembling a cabbage, that is worn at the neck. It may also be placed at the waistline or on a hat.
Collarless — high neckline without a collar, but the garment may have lapels or revers.
Convertible — a straight-edged collar, usually with points, that may be worn open or closed. See Figure 2-11.
Cowl — a soft, bias-cut neckline draped in the front, that was originally introduced by Mme. Vionnet, a French designer. See Figure 2-9.
Cravat (kra-VAHT) — a piece of fabric or a scarf tied around the neck. Cravat is also another name for a necktie.
Crew — a term that comes from the neckline of sweaters worn by rowing crews. It is a round neckline that fits close to the base of the neck.

Detachable — a collar that is removable.
Draped — (see "Dresses").
Eton — (see "Coats, Jackets").
Fichu (FEE shoo) — a collar generally made of a sheer fabric tied in front around the shoulders like a triangular scarf.
Four-in-Hand — a necktie tied with a slipknot, which allows the ends to overlap vertically.
Guimpe (GAMP) — a sleeveless or short-sleeve blouse worn under a dress with a low neckline.
Halter — a sleeveless, backless, bodice held by a strap encircling the neck. See Figure 2-9.
High — a neckline that is high to the throat.
Jabot (zha-BO) — a trimming added to the front of a dress or blouse, originally worn by men. It can be ruffled, pleated, embroidered, or lacy. See Figure 2-11.
Johnny or Band Collar — a stand-up collar similar to a Chinese collar but without the front slit.
Keyhole — a neckline that is usually round and closed at the throat. Below the neckline there is a teardrop-shaped opening. See Figure 2-11.
Lapel — the facing on the front of a garment that folds back across the chest and is attached to the collar. See Figure 2-10.
Middy — (see "Sailor" and Figure 2-11).
Military — a collar adapted from military uniforms, buttoning high on the neck.
Necktie — a band of fabric worn around the neck or under a collar and tied in the front in a knot, bow, or loop.
Notched Lapel — a lapel with a wide, V-shaped space between it and the collar.
Off-the-Shoulder — a neckline that extends over the shoulder line.
Peaked Lapel — a pointed lapel with a narrow space between it and the collar. See Figure 2-10.
Peter Pan — a rounded collar that lies

Clothing Details

flat. It is adapted from the costume worn by Peter Pan in Barrie's play of the same name. See Figure 2-11.

Plastron — a biblike insert worn in place of a collar on the front of a garment.

Plunge — a neckline or collar that dips low in the front, exposing cleavage.

Pointed — a collar with long or short tapered ends.

Puritan — a wide, flat, round collar similar to those worn by the Puritans.

Rever — a turned-back section of a garment exposing the lining or facing, similar to a lapel.

Round or Jewel — a round neckline, either high or low or a round collar of any width.

Ruching (ROO shing) — narrow, decorative fabric, pleated and worn at the neck as a collar.

Ruff — a high, circular collar that is gathered or pleated. It is adapted from costumes of sixteenth and seventeenth century Europe.

Ruffled — any type of collar made from ruffles (see "Construction Details").

Sailor — the traditional collar used on the middy blouse. The sailor collar has a square flap back and slants to a V in front. It is often in a contrasting color to the blouse. See Figure 2-11.

Scarf — an attached or separate piece of fabric, rectangular, square, or triangular, that is tied around the neck.

Shawl — a collar formed like a shawl (see "Coats" and Figure 2-11).

Shirt — a pointed or rounded collar attached to a shirt.

Slotted — a man's shirt collar that has stays on the underside to keep the collar from curling.

Spread — a man's basic shirt collar having points that are spread apart.

Square — a collar or a neckline that has squared-off corners.

Figure 2-10. The V-shaped Space between the Lapel and Collar Is Wider on the Notched Lapel than on the Peaked Lapel.

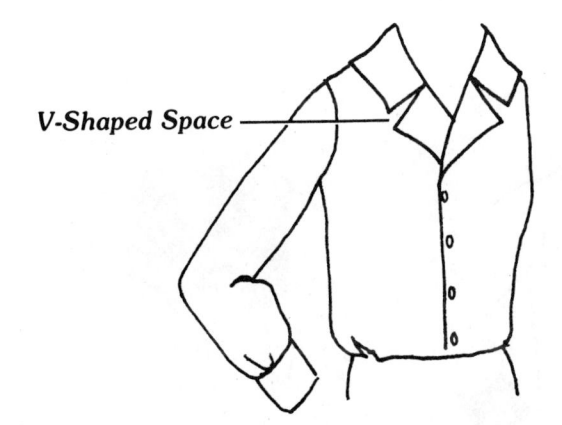

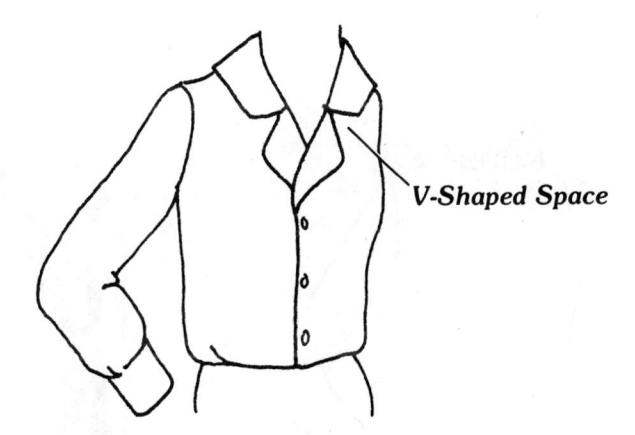

Figure 2-11. Neckline and Collar Styles.

Jabot

Keyhole

Convertible Collar

Shawl Collar

Peter Pan Collar

Surplice

Turtleneck

Middy Blouse

Sailor Collar

Clothing Details

Stock Tie — a wide, straight piece of fabric for wrapping around the neck, with the ends overlapping in front. This was originally worn with riding habits.

Strapless — a dress bodice or blouse that has built-in support, that is, it is not held up by straps.

Surplice (SUR-plis) — a term originally referring only to the white vestment worn over the cassock (long, black garment) of Roman Catholic and Anglican clergy. The term also refers to a V-neckline formed by wrapping one front half of a garment over the other, then fastening it at the side. See Figure 2-11.

Sweetheart — a neckline that forms the top of a heart in the front. It can be high or low.

Tab — a man's shirt collar with attached tabs in front that close to hold the points in place.

Turtleneck — a high, snug collar that is turned or rolled over, commonly used on sweaters. A mock turtleneck gives the same appearance but is not turned over. See Figure 2-11.

Tuxedo — a flat collar that goes around the neck and down the front of a garment without closing. It is used on men's and women's garments.

U-Neck — a neckline that forms a U-shape in the front.

Vandyke — a collar adapted from those in the portraits painted by Anthony Vandyke, a Flemish painter in seventeenth century Europe. It is a broad, pointed collar with a lace edge.

V-neck — a neckline that slants from the shoulders to the center front, forming a V.

Windsor Tie — a man's necktie tied in a double bowknot with the ends overlapping vertically. A half-Windsor is not as wide because it is only knotted once.

Wing — a man's standing collar of stiffened fabric with wing tips, worn for formal occasions.

Sleeves and Cuffs

Barrel or Button Cuff — a single shirt cuff that has a button closing. The simplest cuff has one button, but more exaggerated styles have four or more buttons.

Batwing — a full sleeve with the armhole forming a curve from the waist to the narrow wrist. The term is often used interchangeably with the "Dolman." See Figure 2-12.

Bell — a short or long set-in sleeve that flares into a bell shape from below the cap or armscye. See Figure 2-12.

Bishop — a long set-in sleeve with a narrow cap that increases in width to the cuff where it is gathered. See Figure 2-12.

Cap — a short, kimono sleeve which ends at, or just below, the armhole.

Cape — a sleeve that is a short cape attached at the shoulder. It is open on the underside of the arm. See Figure 2-12.

Convertible Cuff — a single cuff with a buttonhole on each side but with only one button. The cuff can be buttoned or worn with links.

Dolman — a long sleeve for women's coats, suits, or dresses that curves from a wide armhole to a narrow wrist (see "Batwing" and Figure 2-12).

Drop Shoulder — the shoulder line of a coat, jacket, dress, or blouse that extends over the upper arm. A sleeve can be attached. See Figure 2-12.

French Cuff — a double shirt cuff, that is, one that turns back and fastens with links.

Kimono — a sleeve adapted from the Japanese kimono (see "Dresses") that is cut in one piece with the bodice. It has a high underarm, a slight curve over the shoulder, and is best suited for cap sleeves. In order for a longer sleeve that curves under the high underarm to fit well, a gusset must be added (see "Construction Details").

Figure 2-12. Sleeve Styles.

Batwing

Bell

Bishop

Cape

Dolman

Drop Shoulder

Leg-O'-Mutton

Melon

Puff

Raglan

Roll-Up

Shirt Sleeve with Single Cuff

Clothing Details

Lantern — a set-in sleeve which flares from the shoulder to, or near, the elbow, where there is a seam. Below that point, the sleeve tapers into the arm. The shape resembles a Chinese lantern.

Leg-O'-Mutton — a long, set-in sleeve popularized by the Gibson Girl look of the 1890's. The sleeve is gathered for fullness over the shoulder and upper arm, but fits tightly below the elbow. See Figure 2-12.

Melon — a short, full sleeve, usually with gores (see "Construction Details") to give a puffed shape. See Figure 2-12.

Petal — a set-in sleeve that appears to wrap around the arm, with one section overlapping another, forming a petaled effect.

Puff — a set-in sleeve that is gathered at the shoulder for fullness. The short version looks like a melon sleeve. The longer version is full to the wrist, where it is gathered in a tight cuff. See Figure 2-12.

Push-Up — a close-fitting sleeve that is set-in or raglan, that is worn pushed up to, or above, the elbow, rather than at its full length.

Raglan — a coat, jacket, or dress sleeve that is cut to extend to the neckline and thus includes the garment's shoulder. The raglan forms a rounded, narrow shoulder line. See Figure 2-12. The sleeve can be combined with drop-shoulder or princess styling to vary the look. "Saddle shoulder" variation is square cut from the neck across the shoulder.

Ribbed Cuff — a cuff on knitted garments that has raised ridges or wales and is snug-fitting.

Roll-Up — a straight, casual, set-in sleeve that is hemmed and then rolled to the desired length, usually just above the elbow. See Figure 2-12.

Set-In — any sleeve that is sewn or set into a regular armhole. The armhole can be high or low, and the sleeve can be long or short, straight or full.

Shirt — a long, set-in sleeve that is gathered, although it is not full, into either a button, a convertible, or a French cuff. See Figure 2-12.

Sleeveless — a dress, blouse, coat, or jacket that has no sleeves.

Suit — a long, straight, tapered, set-in sleeve, usually with a dart at the elbow for smooth fit.

Construction Details

Appliqué *(ap-li-KAY)* — a piece of fabric in a decorative shape that is sewn or glued to another fabric or garment.

Backing or Underlining — fabric cut, shaped, and sewn to the wrong side of a garment before final construction.

Basting — a temporary row of hand or machine stitching used to hold garment sections together during clothing construction.

Belted — any garment with a belt.

Bias — the true bias on cloth is a 45-degree angle to the warp (lengthwise threads). Garments cut on the bias drape easily, because the bias stretches. Bias-cut fabric is also used when cling is desired (see "Dresses").

Binding — single- or double-fold bias tape, braid, or lace used to finish the raw edges or seams on a garment. It may be sewn or ironed onto the garment.

Braid — a trimming or binding which may be woven, tubular, or plaited.

Button — a fastening or ornament on a garment, usually in the shape of a disk or knob. There are two types of buttons: one that is sewn through the center of the button, and one that is sewn through a shank or stem on the button's underside.

A button used for a fastening closes through a buttonhole slit or loop. Buttons are made in many materials including bone, leather, metal, plastic, shell, and wood. Some are covered in fabric.

Circular — any garment or part of a garment that is cut in a round shape (also includes semicircular).

Cording — a decoration used on apparel made by running a thin cord through a bias strip of fabric and stitching it to a garment at an edge or seam. It can also be put in a tuck.

Cut-and-Sewn — garments that are made from different parts that are cut out and sewn together (as opposed to knitted garments).

Dart — a tuck that is stitched along a line tapering to a point. Darts are used to shape a garment.

Double-Breasted — a garment with two rows of buttons as closures, side by side.

Epaulet (ep-a-LET) — an ornament, often of braid, worn on the shoulders of a coat, jacket, or dress. It was originally worn on military uniforms.

Eyelet — a small hole finished with a buttonhole stitch. It is used as an embroidery decoration or as a hole for lacing.

Facing — a piece of fabric that is either separate and sewn into, or is attached to, the inside edge of a garment to finish, decorate, or support it.

Findings — tools and materials necessary for a workman to produce his product. In clothing construction the findings include scissors, thread, pins, needles, and closures.

Fitted — a garment that lies close to the body, or a garment that has been tried on and altered for fit.

Flounce — a wide, decorative ruffle.

Fly Front — a garment closure that is an overlapping fold of cloth hiding a zipper or other fastenings.

Footing — a lace flounce sewn to cloth, or ½-inch to 3-inch Brussels net that has been inserted.

Fringe — a hanging trim made from threads or cords.

Frog — decorative loop fastening made of braid or cording.

Full Fashioned — a shaped knitted garment made on a flat knitting machine by increasing and decreasing stitches. The term is often used for sweaters.

Gathering — pulling cloth along a thread so as to create small folds or puckers to give controlled fullness in a section of a garment. See Figure 2-14.

Gimp — a ribbonlike trim, often with wire or cord stiffening in the core.

Godet (go-DAY) — a triangular insert added to a garment for flare (usually near the hem).

Gore — a shaped panel added to a dress, shirt, or coat for fullness. A gore is also an elastic panel added to a shoe for ease in putting on and removing the shoe.

Gusset — a shaped piece of material, often triangular, sewn into a garment (usually under the arm) for extra room and strength.

Hem — the raw edge of a garment, usually the bottom edge, which is folded back and stitched. It may be straight, curved, rolled, faced, bound, or piped.

Hook and Eye — a closure consisting of a curved piece of metal wire (the hook) that catches a round or straight loop (the eye).

Interfacing — fabric cut the same as the facing and sewn between the facing and the garment for additional support.

Interlining — fabric cut the same as the lining and sewn between the lining and the garment for warmth.

Lacing — a cord or ribbon that is used for closing shoes and some garments. Two ends of the lacing loop through eyelets or hooks, cross each other, and then loop again until the item is fastened.

Clothing Details

Lining — fabric which is cut, shaped, sewn together, and then attached to the inside of a garment.

Overcasting — a stitching technique used to finish off seams or in embroidery.

Padding — a soft material used to thicken certain parts of a garment such as the shoulders in a jacket or suit. It is also used to give contour in the cups of brassieres and bathing suits.

Paillette (pie-YET) — a small, shiny disk sewn onto fabric or a garment for decoration.

Passementerie (pah-SMEN-tree) — elaborate trimmings, usually made from combinations of gimp, braid, cords, and beads.

Picot (PE-ko) — a small loop of thread used in a series as an edging on ribbon, lace, or a garment.

Pinking — cutting the edge of a fabric or garment in a sawtooth pattern. It is used for decoration and to prevent raveling.

Piping — a piece of fabric, cord, or braid used as trim on the edge or seam of a garment.

Placket — a finished slit in a garment for ease in putting it on and removing it. Zippers, buttons, hooks, and snaps are usually put into a placket.

Pleats — folds of fabric that are usually pressed or stitched in place to add fullness to a garment. There are many different kinds of pleats, as shown in Figure 2-13:

1. **Accordian** — thin, even pleats, one folded over another like the bellows of an accordian.
2. **Box** — two knife pleats folded to face each other on the wrong side of the garment.

Figure 2-13. Kinds of Pleating.

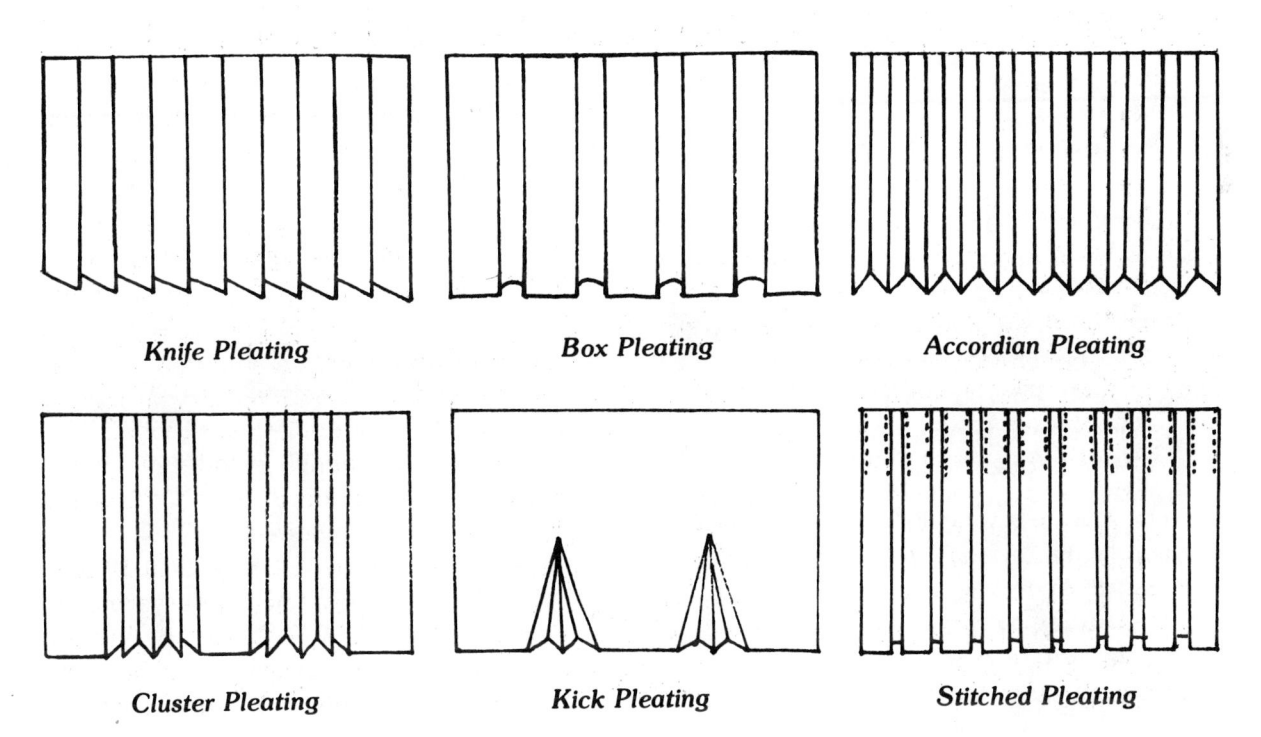

Knife Pleating

Box Pleating

Accordian Pleating

Cluster Pleating

Kick Pleating

Stitched Pleating

3. **Cartridge** — pleats with a rounded top, giving a tubular effect.
4. **Cluster** — a grouping of several types of soft pleats (excluding knife pleats).
5. **Inverted** — two knife pleats folded away from each other on the wrong side of the garment.
6. **Kick** — similar to an inverted pleat, a kick pleat is usually placed low on a straight garment to give extra room for movement.
7. **Knife** — narrow pleats all turned in the same direction, usually right to left, around the body.
8. **Stitched-Down** — pleats which have been sewn from the waist to the hip on either the right side or the wrong side for a smooth fit over the hipline.
9. **Sunburst** — pleats which increase in width from the top of the pleat to the bottom for a fan or sunburst effect.
10. **Unpressed** — pleats that are folded but are neither pressed nor stitched down.

Pocket — a pouchlike piece of fabric sewn into or onto a garment for decoration or for carrying small articles. There are several kinds of pockets:

1. **Patch Pocket** — pocket stitched onto the face of a garment.
2. **Set-In Pocket** — pocket inside a special opening on a garment.
3. **Pocket Set into a Seam** — pocket that has an opening on the seam with the pouch stitched behind it.
4. **Slash Pocket** — a pocket on the inside of the garment with a slashed and flapped opening on the outside.

Quilting — sewing soft padding between two layers of fabric. It is usually done in crossed lines or in a pattern.

Repoussé (reh-poo-SAY) — patterns made by raising fabric or leather in relief on the face of the garment.

Reversible — a fabric or garment which can be used on either side.

Ribbon — narrow strips of woven fabric with finished selvages, often tied, that are used for trimming or decorating.

Rickrack — a decorative woven trim that forms a sawtooth pattern.

Ruche (ROOSH) — a pleated or frilled piece of lace, ribbon, or decorative fabric used as a trimming.

Ruffle — a narrow, gathered, pleated piece of fabric used as a trim. See Figure 2-14.

Seam — the line formed when two pieces of fabric are sewn or joined together to form parts of a garment. Seams can be sewn by hand or by machine. There are many different kinds of seams:

1. **Corded** — a plain seam with a strip of cording sewn into it on the right side of the garment, similar to the piped seam.
2. **Flat Fell** — a plain seam used for men's shirts, pajamas, and sportswear. After a plain seam is sewn with wrong sides together, one seam allowance is trimmed, the other is folded over it, and they are topstitched to the garment.
3. **French** — a double seam used primarily on sheer fabrics. A plain seam is stitched on the right side of the fabric and is trimmed and pressed. Then the fabric is turned right sides together, and a second seam is made, enclosing the raw edges of the first.
4. **Lapped** — a seam used on yokes and gussets. The seam allowance of the added part (yoke or gusset) is folded under. It is then placed with right sides up over the seam allowance of the main piece and sewn together.
5. **Piped** — a decorative seam that has a piece of piping sewn between the seam edges on the right side of a

Clothing Details

garment. The piping is usually contrasting.

6. **Plain** — the most common seam, used to join the parts of a garment. The edges of the garment sections to be joined are lined up, right sides of fabric together, then the seam is stitched on the wrong side and pressed open.
7. **Saddle Stitching** — a decorative, hand-topstitched seam, often done on leather with contrasting thread.
8. **Slot** — a decorative seam with a contrasting piece of fabric showing through. The seam allowances from the two edges to be joined are folded under to form tucks. The contrasting piece of fabric is inserted under the tucks, and the tucks are stitched to it.
9. **Topstitched** — a plain seam which has a row of hand stitching or machine stitching on the right side. A double topstitched seam has a row of stitching on both sides of the plain seam.
10. **Welt** — a seam used for sportswear and heavy fabrics. A plain seam is stitched with the right sides together, then pressed open. One seam allowance is trimmed, and the other is folded over it and stitched to the garment.

Selvage — the finished "self-edge" which runs lengthwise, or warpwise, on both edges of woven fabric. The selvage keeps the cloth straight and even, and prevents it from raveling. Selvage also refers to the finished edge on knitted cloth.

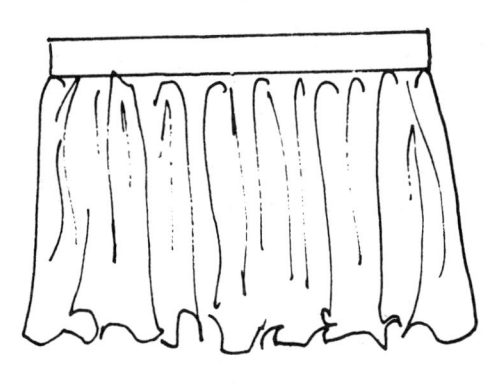

Figure 2-14. Stitching Effects.

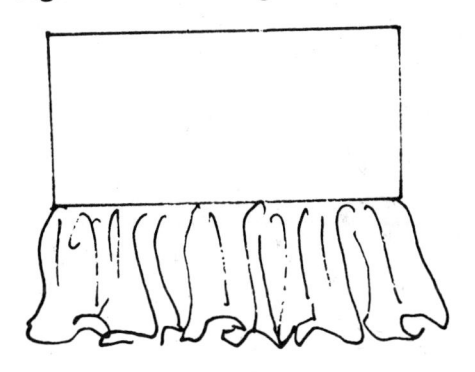

Gathering

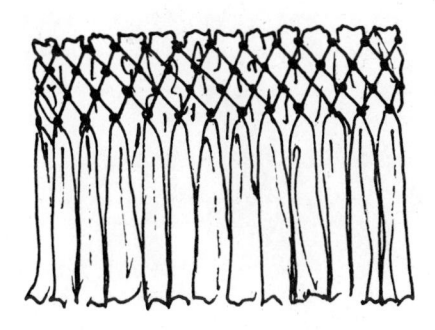

Ruffling

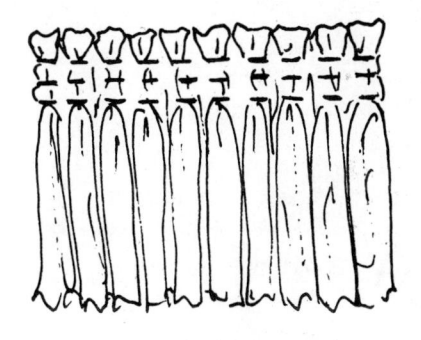

Smocking

Shirring

Semi-Fitted — a garment that does not precisely follow the contour of the body.
Shirring — a series of parallel rows of running stitches that are drawn together to form gathers. See Figure 2-14.
Single-Breasted — a garment with one row of buttons down the front as the closure.
Smocking — rows of decorative stitching in a honeycomb pattern that hold fullness in place evenly on a garment. See Figure 2-14.
Snaps — a two-piece circular metal or fabric-covered closure used on garment sections where there is light stress. One piece has a small ball in the center that is pressed into a hole on the other piece.
Soutache *(soo-TASH)* — a flat, narrow braid used as trimming.
Tiers — rows of ruffles or flounces on a garment layered one on top of another.
Trapunto — a type of quilting with a high, raised design. Each part of the pattern is outlined with stitches and padded separately.
Tuck — a small fold that is stitched in place. It is used to hold fullness, to shorten, to shape, or to decorate. A pin tuck is a very small tuck, usually used in a series for decoration.
Yoke — a separate section of fabric set into a garment, usually to support pleats or gathers. The yoke in a bodice extends from the shoulders to a seam right above the bustline. A shirt may have a yoke in the back or, as in a Western-styled shirt, a yoke in both the front and back. Pants and skirts can have a yoke from the waistband to the hipline.
Zipper — a closure consisting of a sliding tab on a track of teeth or coil. A zipper is usually set in a placket.

Clothing Details

Projects For Clothing Details

1. From current newspapers and fashion magazines, find illustrations of five different silhouettes in each of the categories listed below. Include samples of men's, women's, and children's wear. Label the illustrations using the terms in this chapter and mount the illustrations in your notebook.

   A. Dresses and Skirts
   B. Jackets and Coats
   C. Blouses and Shirts
   D. Pants
   E. Collars and Necklines
   F. Sleeves

2. Design five original garments in each of the categories listed below. Label each design stating the clothing details you used (for example, pants suit with braid trim, or Norfolk jacket and cuffed flare pants).

   A. Men's wear
   B. Women's wear
   C. Children's wear

Bibliography

Fashion Dictionary: Fabric, Sewing, and Apparel As Expressed in the Language of Fashion. Edited by Mary Brooks Picken. New York: Funk & Wagnalls, 1972.

Wilcox, R. Turner. ***The Dictionary of Costume.*** New York: Charles Scribner's Sons, 1963.

Wingate, Isabel B., Gillespie, Karen R., and Addison, Betty G. ***Know Your Merchandise.*** 4th ed. New York: McGraw-Hill Book Co., 1975.

3

Outline of Costume History

Fashion is an evolutionary process. Every new style is an adaptation or an extension of a previous style. For this reason, clothing is studied from a historical viewpoint. To illustrate, the silhouette of a period garment, such as a Roman toga, might be adapted for a current design, and a style detail, such as the broad padded shoulders of 1930's clothes, might be used.

Men and women have been wearing clothing since prehistoric times when they first covered themselves with animal skins for protection from the elements. Earliest use of clothing was also for the purpose of adornment. Costume changes have been documented since the times of the ancient cultures in the Fertile Crescent of the Middle East. Over the centuries, information about the costume of a culture or a period has been found in sculpture, statues, painted pottery, tomb paintings, scrolls, architecture, paintings, reliefs, historical and philosophical writings, novels, stories, newspapers, magazines, and photographs.

This chapter is an outline of the important costume styles from 3000 B.C. to A.D. 1947, presenting a broad scope of fashion changes over the centuries. You will see how styles throughout history have influenced today's styles. The number of terms and their unfamiliarity may seem overwhelming at first scan of the chapter, but it is not necessary to memorize the descriptions; rather, learn to recognize how costume changed throughout the ages.

There are two historical time lines in the chapter (see Figures 3-1 and 3-2). They show how cultures and periods overlap. The first time line traces the progress of the ancient civilizations, starting in 3000 B.C. and continuing to the Renaissance. The second begins in A.D. 1600 and continues to just after World War II.

Egyptian

Schenti (SHEN-tee) — a loincloth worn by men of all classes. In the period of the Middle Kingdom, the schenti was often pleated, or adorned with a triangular projection in front. See Figure 3-3.

Kalasiris (ka-la-SEE-ris) — a long, slim, woven or knitted garment worn by men and women. The traditional kalasiris hung from the breasts to the ankles and was held by one or two straps going over the shoulders. It was often transparent and worn over a schenti or skirt. During

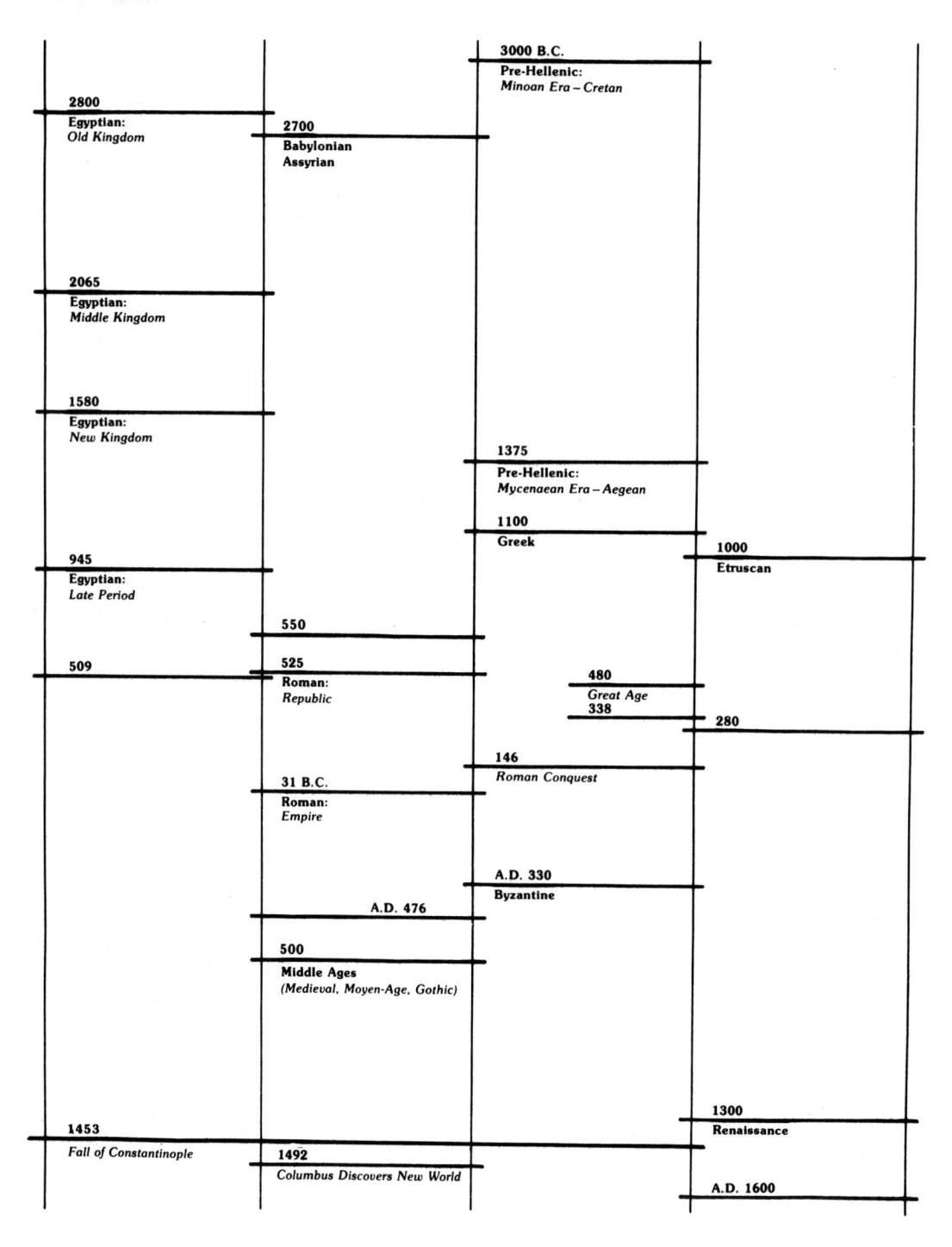

Figure 3-1. Costume History Time Line, part 1. This two-part time line is a flow chart to be read from top to bottom. It shows beginning and ending dates, as well as simultaneous events.

```
                                3000 B.C.
                                Pre-Hellenic:
                                Minoan Era – Cretan
2800
Egyptian:          2700
Old Kingdom        Babylonian
                   Assyrian




2065
Egyptian:
Middle Kingdom



1580
Egyptian:
New Kingdom
                                1375
                                Pre-Hellenic:
                                Mycenaean Era – Aegean
                                1100
945                             Greek          1000
Egyptian:                                      Etruscan
Late Period
                   550
509                525                480
                   Roman:              Great Age
                   Republic            338
                                                280
                                146
                   31 B.C.      Roman Conquest
                   Roman:
                   Empire

                                A.D. 330
                                Byzantine
                   A.D. 476
                   500
                   Middle Ages
                   (Medieval, Moyen-Age, Gothic)



                                               1300
1453                                           Renaissance
Fall of Constantinople    1492
                          Columbus Discovers New World
                                               A.D. 1600
```

Outline of Costume History

Figure 3-2. Costume History Time Line, Part 2.

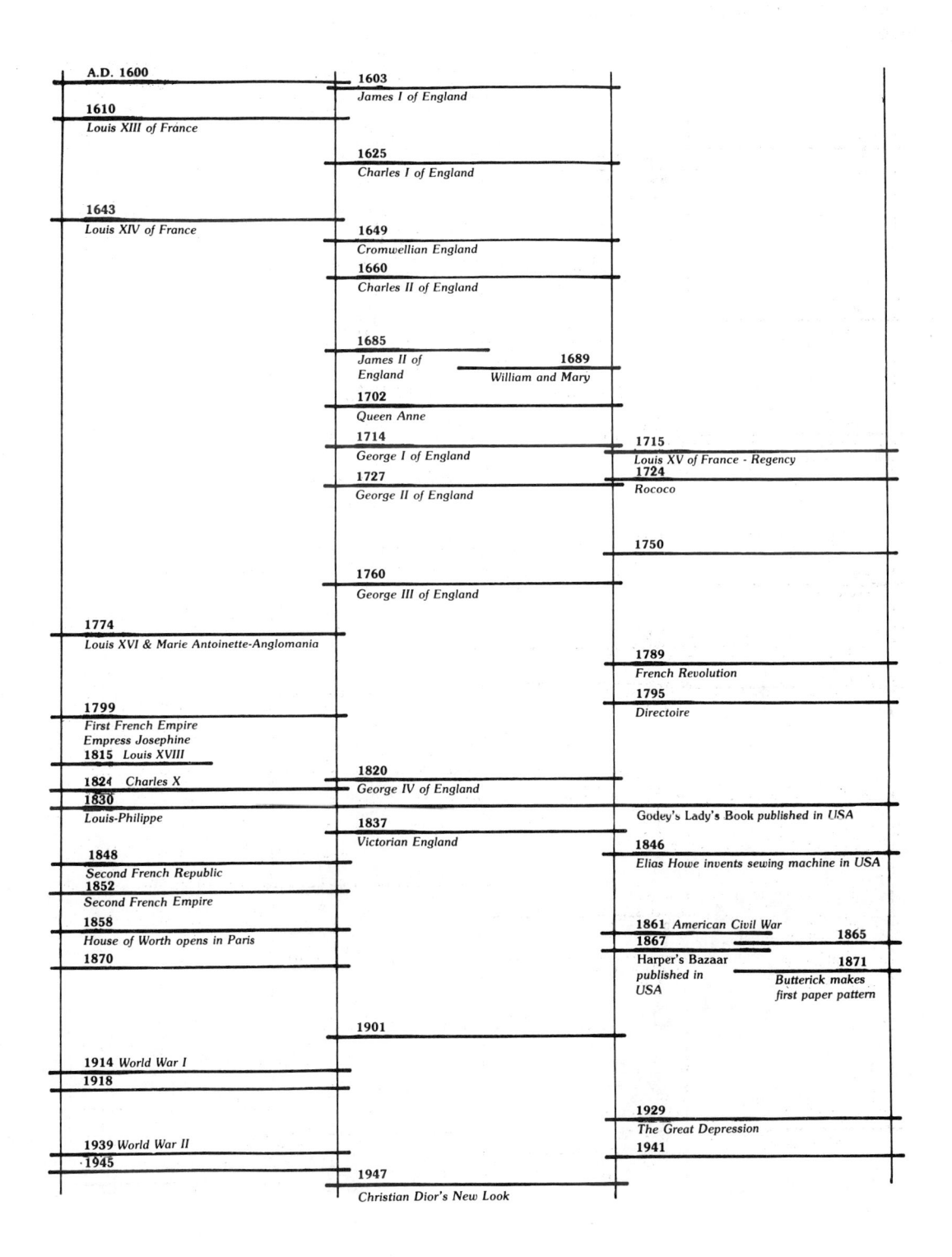

France	England	Other
A.D. 1600	1603 James I of England	
1610 Louis XIII of France		
	1625 Charles I of England	
1643 Louis XIV of France	1649 Cromwellian England	
	1660 Charles II of England	
	1685 James II of England	1689 William and Mary
	1702 Queen Anne	
	1714 George I of England	1715 Louis XV of France - Regency
	1727 George II of England	1724 Rococo
		1750
	1760 George III of England	
1774 Louis XVI & Marie Antoinette-Anglomania		1789 French Revolution
1799 First French Empire Empress Josephine		1795 Directoire
1815 Louis XVIII		
1824 Charles X	1820 George IV of England	
1830 Louis-Philippe	1837 Victorian England	Godey's Lady's Book published in USA
1848 Second French Republic		1846 Elias Howe invents sewing machine in USA
1852 Second French Empire		
1858 House of Worth opens in Paris		1861 American Civil War 1865
1870		1867 Harper's Bazaar published in USA 1871 Butterick makes first paper pattern
	1901	
1914 World War I		
1918		
		1929 The Great Depression
1939 World War II		1941
1945	1947 Christian Dior's New Look	

47

the New Kingdom and Late Period, sleeves were added. See Figure 3-3.

The shoes of this period were simple sandals with turned-up toes, made of papyrus, palm leaves, or leather. Elaborate gold jewelry laden with gems, worn especially as collars and bracelets, adorned the clothing of royalty. Men and women shaved their heads and wore decorative wigs or headdresses. The wigs were heavy, usually black, and were straight or curled. Headdresses were either a

Figure 3-3. Egyptian Costumes.

Ancient Egypt: Kalasiris

*Ancient Egypt:
Schenti with Triangular Projection*

high hat or a triangular, scarflike covering. Men also wore short, braided or jeweled chin beards, attached to the head by gold straps. Women's cosmetics included green and black kohl for the eyes, carmine for the lips, and henna stain for the fingernails. The most important clothing color was white because linen, the primary fiber used for Egyptian clothing, could not be dyed with permanent colors.

Babylonian-Assyrian

Kandys — originally a man's short skirt of goatskin or sheepskin with the hair left intact for decoration. Later it became a wrap-around skirt with fringe. The kandys developed further into a long skirt with a rolled belt, worn by men and women. See Figure 3-4.
Kaunace — a long skirt that was adapted from the kandys. It was generally fringed or embroidered.

The style of hair for men and women of this period was long, and bushy, curly, or braided. Men had long beards. Babylonian men wore turbans or conical hats; Assyrian men wore conical hats, but with a spike on top. Bracelets and jeweled dog collar necklaces were the most popular types of jewelry.

Pre-Hellenic

Men wore heavily patterned loincloths, and hats with round crowns and feather plumes. Women wore bell-shaped, tiered skirts with aprons, and turbans on top of their long hair that was intertwined with beads or bands. A short, close-fitting jacket that exposed the breasts was worn as a bodice (see Figure 3-4). By the Aegean period the women's flounced skirts and the men's loincloths had a hem that dipped in the front. Sandals or half-boots dressed the feet.

Greek

Chiton (KI-tin) — a rectangular garment with or without a girdle (belt or sash), worn by both sexes. The Doric chiton, usually of wool, was worn short by men, boys, and young girls, and was folded over one or both shoulders and pinned. See Figure 3-5. The Ionic chiton, usually of cotton or linen, had no overfold and was pinned along the shoulders and arms to form sleeves.
Peplos — a loose, rectangular garment worn by Doric women over the chiton. It was pinned at the shoulders, open at the sides, and then gathered or bloused with a girdle. The folds were weighted with lead. See Figure 3-5.
Chlamys (CLAM-is) — a short, rectangular, woolen cloak worn by men, clasped on the right shoulder or in front.
Himation (him-AT-ee-an) — a long, rectangular cloak worn by men and women, usually draped over one shoulder. When worn without any undergarments, it was girdled at the waistline. See Figure 3-6.
Petasos (PET-a-sis) — a man's wide-brimmed hat made of straw or felt.
Strophium — a band of fabric or soft skin that women wore over the chiton. It was wrapped below the bust.
Fibulae — decorative pins or clasps used to fasten garments.

Etruscan

Tunic — a robelike garment with closed sides. Men wore short tunics similar to

50 Fashion: Color, Line, and Design

Greek chitons. Women wore longer, close-fitting tunics. Sometimes the tunics had patterned borders.

Tebanna — a semicircular woolen cape worn by men and women.
Tutulus — a conical hat worn by men

Figure 3-4. Babylonian and Pre-Hellenic Costumes.

Babylonian Kandys

Cretan Tiered Skirt and Open-Bodice Jacket

Outline of Costume History　　　　　　　　　　　　　　　　　　　　　　　51

and women. Men also wore the petasos (see Greek).

Footwear — short laced boots with turned-up toes were worn, then later sandals were worn.

Roman

Tunica — a short undergarment with sleeves, worn by men and women. See Figure 3-6.

Figure 3-5. Greek Costumes.

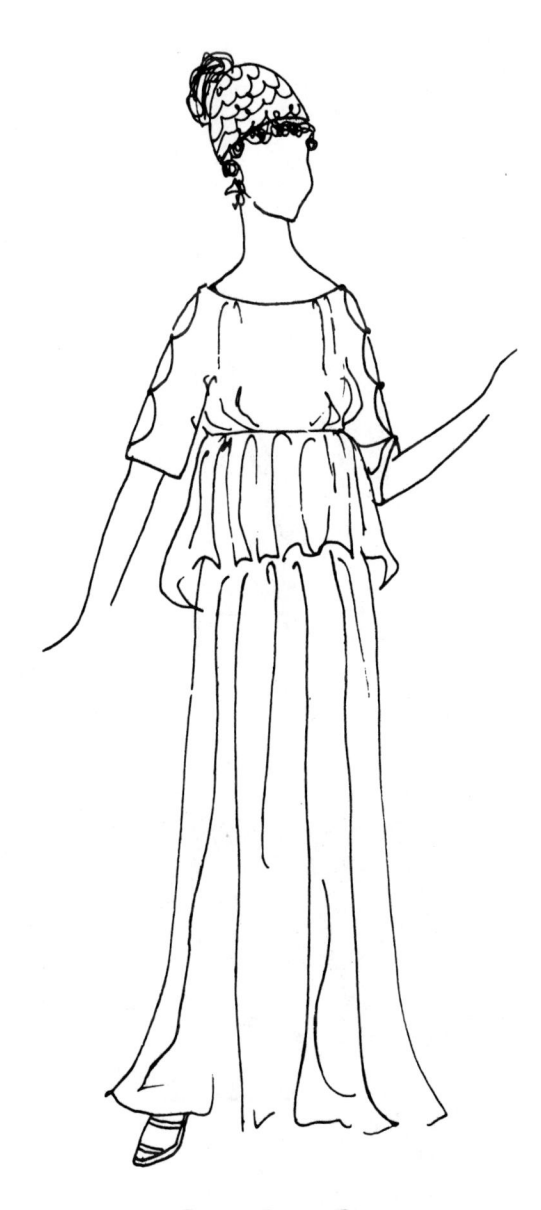

Greek Doric Chiton

Greek Peplos over Chiton

Stola — long, straight linen or woolen overdress with sleeves, worn by women. It was usually bordered with colored embroidery.

Toga — a woolen, elliptical-shaped outer garment worn by male Roman citizens. It was folded vertically, then draped around the body and over the left shoulder or arm.

Toga Pura or Toga Virilis — an undecorated white toga; the toga of the Roman citizen.

Toga Praetexta — a white toga with a red or purple edge, worn by boys

Figure 3-6. Greek and Roman Costumes.

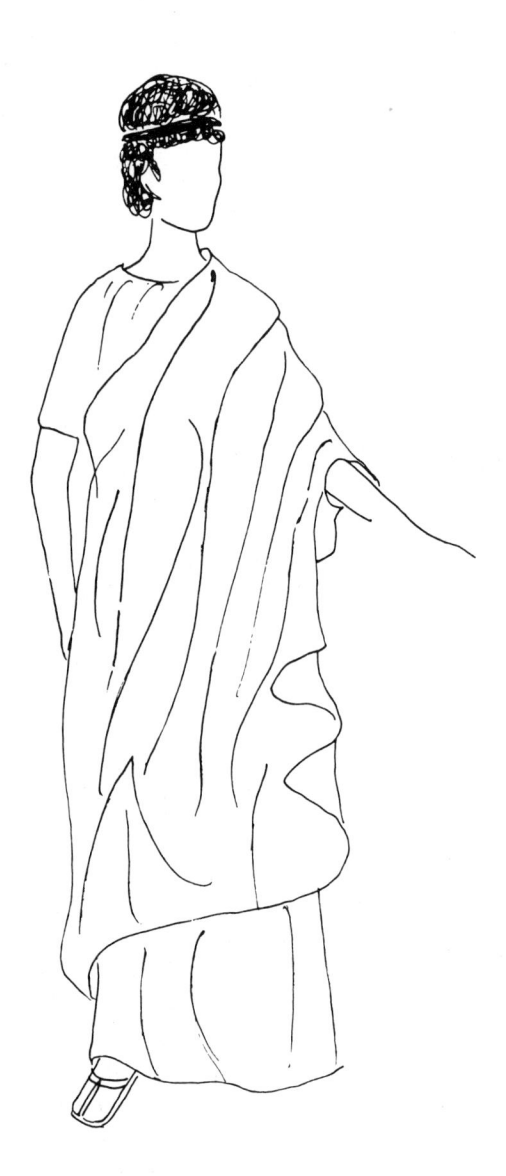

Greek Himation

Roman Toga Praetexta over Tunica

under 16, magistrates, and priests. See Figure 3-6.

Toga Pulla — a black or dark-colored toga worn for mourning.

Toga Picta — a purple toga with gold embroidery, worn by later emperors and consuls.

Pallium — a large, woolen cloak worn by men, draped like the Greek himation. The Pallium, with no additional clothing, was often the attire of the scholar or philosopher.

Palla — a rectangular, woolen cloak that was wrapped. Women used the palla to cover their heads. It could also serve as a bed covering.

Paenula (PEE-nya-la) — a poncholike garment made of wool or leather, sometimes with an attached hood, adapted from an Etruscan cloak. It was pulled on over the head and open at the neck. The Paenula was originally used for inclement weather. By the second century, it replaced the toga.

Strophium — (see Greek).

Footwear for this period was sandals for both men and women. Upper-class citizens decorated themselves with jewelry and used many cosmetics: bath oils, ointments, rouge, powder, perfume, pumice for teeth, and beauty-mark patches. Women's hair styles were first very simple then, during the Empire, became elaborate through the use of curling irons, and veils, combs, and bands. Men's hair was also curled with the curling iron, and men often wore beards. Laurel wreaths adorned the heads of the upper class.

Byzantine

Camisia — a shirtlike tunic with long sleeves, usually worn as an undergarment. It was short for men and long for women.

Dalmatica — a long robe with long, loose sleeves. It was usually worn ungirdled or girdled high on the body. Embroidered stripes called "clavi" decorated the front and back.

Tablion — a long, semicircular cloak adapted from the toga. It was elaborately embroidered and jeweled in squares on the front edges and on the center back edge. It was fastened on the right shoulder with a decorative fibula (see Greek).

Juppe — a short tunic with dolman sleeves (see "Clothing Details: Sleeves"), worn by women in the later part of the Byzantine period.

Rich ornamentation, particularly gold and pearl jewelry and embroidery were used on Byzantine garments. Sandals were worn, but a soft leather ankle-length boot with a pointed toe was more popular.

Middle Ages

Braccae (BRA-ki) — men's long trousers worn by Gauls and Britons. They usually had a drawstring waist.

Chausses (SHOWS) — cloth stockings worn by men.

Chainse (SHANZ) — a tunic worn by men and women as an undergarment. The Britons called this tunic a "shert." It eventually became the chemise.

Bliaud (BLEE-o) — a tunic that appeared in the eleventh century worn by men and women as an outer garment. It had long sleeves, a full skirt, and was usually belted. The bliaud (also bliaut, or bliaus) was the forerunner of the blouse.

Surcoat, Surcot or Surcote (SIR-coat) — by the thirteenth century the surcoat replaced the blouse as an outer garment. It was adapted from a covering the Crusaders wore over their armor to reflect heat. It began as a sleeveless garment with an opening for the head, then, in the woman's surcoat, extra fullness was added with godets (see "Construction Details"), and long, full sleeves were attached. By the fourteenth century, the surcoat was open on the sides to reveal an underdress. See Figure 3-7.

Figure 3-7. Middle Ages Costumes.

*Middle Ages:
Surcoat over Girdled Cotehardie.
Caul Headdress and Toque*

*Middle Ages:
Houppelande with Fur.
Hennin Headdress*

Cote or Cotte (COAT) — a garment with a tight bodice, long sleeves, a girdle, and a full skirt worn by men and women. The woman's cote was long and often laced up the front.

Cotehardie (CODE-ar-dee) — worn by men and women from the twelfth through the fourteenth century. The man's cotehardie was a short, close-fitting jacket with a buttoned front, long sleeves, and a low girdle. The woman's version was similarly styled, but with a long full skirt. Women wore surcoats with side openings over the cotehardie. See Figure 3-7.

Pourpoint (POOR-point) — a man's quilted jacket worn from the thirteenth to the seventeenth century in place of the surcoat.

Pelisse (peh-LEES) — a coat originally worn by women during the twelfth to the fifteenth century. It was knee length and loose, with flowing sleeves. The pelisse was often lined with fur for warmth (ermine was the most desired fur).

Houppelande (HUH-pland) — a coat-like garment for men and women. The houppelande was originally Germanic and was worn throughout Europe from the fourteenth to the sixteenth century. It was long (although men also wore a short version), girdled at the waist, and had flowing sleeves. It was often lined with fur for warmth. See Figure 3-7.

Chaperon (SHAP-a-rone) — a short cape with a hood, worn by men from the twelfth to the sixteenth century. By the fourteenth century, the chaperon had developed into a turbanlike headdress. See Figure 3-8.

Liripipe (LIR-i-pipe) — a long point or tail extending from the top of the chaperon to varying lengths. The longest liripipes almost touched the floor. The liripipe could be wrapped around or folded on top of the headdress. See Figure 3-8.

Roundlet — a turbanlike hat adapted from the chaperon. It was made over a round, stuffed roll. A liripipe was often added for decoration.

Wimple — a square, rectangular, or circular piece of cloth, usually linen, worn as a woman's headdress. It was held in place by a fabric-covered metal band or a crown, and often a chinband was worn with it. The wimple may be worn today as a part of the nun's habit. It is also called a "headrail" or "couvrechef."

Caul (CALL) — a woman's headpiece made of silk, metallic cord, and jewels, covering the hair, having a netlike appearance. A crown or wimple was often worn over it.

Hennin — a tall, conical headdress worn by women. It was supported by a small skullcap and frontlet over the forehead. A veil was often attached to the hennin. See Figure 3-7.

Escoffion (es-COF-ee-on) — a variation of the hennin headdress, shaped to form two horns with veils attached.

Aumônière (oh-mun-YARE) — a small, drawstring bag made of leather or fabric that hung from the girdle. It was worn by men and women. See Figure 3-8.

Baldric (BALL-drik) — a leather or fabric sash worn by men diagonally from the left shoulder to the right hip then around the body back to the left shoulder. Tiny silver bells often hung from the baldric. See Figure 3-8.

Poulaines (POO-lanes) or Crackowes (KRAH-kows) — shoes that originated in Cracow, Poland, in the fourteenth century that were worn by European men through the fifteenth century. The shoes were of fabric or soft leather and had a long, pointed toe. The points reached extreme lengths, as much as 18 inches, and noblemen often had gold chains attached from the points to their knees. Laws were finally passed regulating the length of the points. See Figure 3-8.

Pattens — wood or cork clogs strapped to the bottom of men's and women's soft shoes to protect the soles of the feet.

Figure 3-8. Middle Ages Costumes.

Middle Ages: Chaperon with Liripipe over Parti-Colored Cotehardie with Castellated Edges, Parti-Colored Hose, and Poulaines. Aumônière on Girdle

Middle Ages: Surcoat with Coat-of-Arms, Baldric, and Girdle over Hauberk

Chopines (cho-PEEN) — a Turkish wooden shoe made on stilts and painted. It was adopted by Venetian women in the sixteenth century.

Parti-Colored — divided into contrasting colors. Much of the men's and women's clothing of the fourteenth and fifteenth centuries was designed in this way. The family coats of arms were often incorporated onto the parti-colored garments. See Figure 3-8.

Hauberk (HAW-berk) — a coat of chain mail or armor. See Figure 3-8.

Castellated — an edging used on men's and women's apparel similar to a scallop except that the edges were cut square (see "Design Motifs: Embattled Border" and Figure 3-8).

Renaissance

Doublet or Jerkin — the Middle Age man's pourpoint became the Renaissance man's doublet. It was a short, padded jacket, sometimes with a peplum (see "Clothing Details: Skirts").

Peasecodbelly Doublet — a doublet originating in fifteenth century Spain. The front was greatly exaggerated with padding and wooden supports. See Figure 3-9.

Trunk Hose — men's short breeches of the sixteenth century laced to doublet and stockings. Trunk hose were puffed and often slashed. See Figure 3-9.

Venetians — men's full breeches that were tied below the knee. They originated in Italy.

Codpiece — a small pouch laced to trunk hose or breeches to cover the front opening. See Figure 3-9.

Canions (CAN-yenz) — breeches of knee length, originating in France when trunk hose became very short. Canions were often made with puffs and slashes.

Basquine (bah-SKEEN) — a woman's tight-fitting corset originating in France. It had a low, square neckline and was made of metal rods covered with fabric.

Vertingale or Vertugadin — a bell-shaped canvas underskirt with a wicker hoop of Spanish origin that became popular in France.

Farthingale (FAR-thin-gale) — a hoop underskirt of Spanish origin that was popular in Elizabethan England. The hoop was very wide over the hips and formed an exaggerated elliptical (oval) shape. Fabric draped vertically from the hoop to the floor. See Figure 3-9.

Stomacher — a decorative panel that dipped to a front point below the waist, made with metal or boned stays covered in fabric (busks). It was worn by men and women. See Figure 3-9.

Marolotte (mar-o-LUT) — a long, loose cloak with a stand-up collar worn by women over the gown.

Ruff — a stiff, circular collar worn by men and women that was pleated, gathered, wired, or starched to stand away from the neckline. Some ruffs looked like cartwheels. See Figure 3-9.

Medici Collar — a high, standing, fan-shaped collar with a décolletage. It was worn by Marie de Medici, wife of Henri IV of France.

Conch — a cloak worn by women that was wired into the shape of a conch shell from the waist up. It usually covered the head and shoulders.

Gable Hood — a headdress worn by English women that was wired to form a gable peak. It had a piece of fabric that fell to the shoulders in back.

Beret — a round, cloth cap without a visor. Berets of this period were large or small and some were stiff, but most were very soft. They were worn by men and women, and plumes often accented the hats. See Figure 3-9.

Toque — a velvet cap with a full crown and a small rolled brim worn by men and women.
Ferronière (fer-en-YARE) — a thin ribbon or chain that was worn by women around the head and had a jeweled pendant that rested on the forehead.
Pantoffle (PAN-te-fel) — a cork-soled

Figure 3-9. Renaissance Costumes.

Renaissance: Peascodbelly Doublet with Slashings over Trunk Hose with Codpiece. Feather-Trimmed Beret

Renaissance: Elizabethan Farthingale with Stomacher and Ruff

covering for the instep with a front piece. Pantoffles were pulled on over soft slippers for outdoor wear.

Women of this period wore gowns with tight-fitting, low-cut bodices, full skirts over stuffed petticoats, and long slim or leg-o'-mutton sleeves (see "Clothing Details: Sleeves"). Men's shoes no longer had long, pointed toes, but were rounded or squared at the toe. Women wore low-cut pumps or slippers with a high heel. Masks, muffs, and fans, and jeweled and perfumed gloves were important accessories worn by men and women.

Seventeenth Century

In the beginning of the seventeenth century, the man's stiff doublet became softer, with a longer front point and a longer skirt, and the slashes revealed a lingerie shirt underneath. By 1640 the doublet had turned into a short jacket with sleeves and buttons — the *bolero*. Folds of the shirt were visible between the bolero hem and breeches. Breeches were still attached to the doublet at the start of the century, were no longer padded, and were cut narrow and to the knee.

In the latter part of the century, men wore longer jackets that hugged the body, had buttons, were collarless, and had sleeves with turned-back cuffs. This longer jacket was the forerunner of the waistcoat.

Rhinegraves or Petticoat Breeches — a short full skirt, very fancy and often divided, which covered full knee breeches. Rhinegraves were popular during the middle of the century. See Figure 3-10.
Vandyke or Falling Band Collar — a white collar made of lawn (fine, thin fabric of cotton or linen) trimmed with lace, that lay flat on the shoulders. It was popular for men and women during the middle of the century.
Cravat — a folded piece of white fabric with lace trim for men, that was tied around the neck. The cravat dates from the middle of the century.
Cavalier — the term used to describe the elegant man of the seventeenth century.
Cassock — a man's loose coat with long sleeves, turned back cuffs, and buttons.
Cannons — a linen and lace ruffled tube worn by men underneath the petticoat breeches.
Steinkirk — a man's neck scarf that became popular at the end of the century. It was made of lace, lawn, or black silk. The ends were tucked inside the shirt or pulled through a ring.
Tricorne — a three-cornered hat for gentlemen, popular for an entire century. The tricorne was a later form of the wide-brimmed hat cocked in three places. Women adapted the tricorne style for their hats.

The stiff, padded look for men gave way to the looser look of *The Three Musketeers*. Long capes with sleeves and collars, boots with heels and wide tops that were folded over, and stiff hats made of felt or beaver, with wide brims that were cocked and plumes best characterize this period. Elaborate baldrics were also worn to hold the sword in place (see "Middle Ages: Baldric").

In women's wear the hoop-skirted gown of the Renaissance gave way to a short-waisted overskirt with an opening in the skirt front. The opening revealed a contrasting underskirt and stomacher. Numerous petticoats made the skirt stand out from the body, and many skirts had trains. Low necklines were popular, as were collars. Collars evolved from the standing ruff at the beginning of the century, to the Vandyke in the middle of the century, to scarf collars toward the end of the century.

In the latter part of the century, women gathered and pinned the overskirt in various ways. In the 1670's overskirts were gathered up at the sides to form panels that looked like panniers (see below). Later, a wire frame or a pad was attached at the back, and the skirt was looped over it to form a bustle.

Pannier (PAN-yare) — a hoop worn under skirts toward the end of the cen-

Figure 3-10. Seventeenth Century Costumes.

1660's: Bolero Jacket, Lingerie Shirt over Rhinegrave Breeches. Brimmed Hat with Feathers.

1670's: Gown with Panniers and Echelle Panel

tury. It was an exaggerated version of the farthingale and extended straight out from the waistline with a flat front and back. See Figure 3-10.

Pinners — a small, decorative apron worn on top of the underskirt and seen at the front opening of the overskirt.

Transparents — sheer painted or lace gowns worn over another gown during the middle of the century.

Palatine — a small woman's cape originally made of fur. It was brought to France in the 1670's by the Princess Palatine, who married Le Duc d'Orleans, the brother of King Louis XIV. Palatine later referred to a fur scarf.

Echelle (ah-SHELL) — a stiffened panel with rows of ribbon tied in bows, worn on the front of the bodice usually over, or as, a stomacher. "Echelle" is the French word for *ladder*. See Figure 3-10.

Galants — loops of multi-colored ribbon worn by men and women on their clothes and in their hair, and attached to walking sticks.

Falbalas (FAL-ba-laz) — rows of heavy ruffles worn on gowns in the late years of the century, also known as "furbelows" (FUR-ba-lowz).

Prentintailles (pran-teen-TAY) — lace or embroidered appliqués worn in the late years of the century.

Fontange (fone-TAZH) — a woman's headdress made of tiers of stiffened lace ruffles and ribbons attached to a cap. It was originated by the Duchesse de Fontanges in 1680.

Periwig — an elaborate wig, very popular during the century, often powdered, perfumed, or jeweled. It was also called "perruque" or "peruke."

Lavallière — a necklace with a pendant adapted from the pendants worn by Louise de la Vallière, the first mistress of King Louis XIV.

Temple Jewels — costume jewelry made on Rue de Temple in France.

Important accessories of the seventeenth century included face powder, rouge, decorative face patches, fans, gloves, handkerchiefs, sashes, buttons, snuff boxes, muffs, walking sticks, umbrellas, rosettes, and boutonnieres.

Men and women wore soft leather or fabric shoes with heels and soles. The toe was usually square or rounded. The high (Louis) heel was curved, and heels were often red. Buckles, rosettes, ribbons, and embroidery decorated the shoes. High-heeled pantoffles were also worn.

Eighteenth Century

During the eighteenth century France became the fashion leader. Except for the last twenty years in the century, when it was greatly influenced by England (during "anglomania"), France remained the most important fashion country in Europe.

Habit á la Française — a combination of coat, vest, and breeches for men. For the first half of the eighteenth century, the skirts of the knee-length coats had exaggerated fullness at the hips. A lingerie chemise was worn with a cravat or jabot (see "Clothing Details: Collars") at the neck. Breeches were close-fitting and ended above the knee with stockings rolled over them. The breeches were lengthened to reach below the knee during the reign of Louis XVI.

Frac (frok) — a man's coat that was worn in the second half of the century. The fullness was in the back, and the front was cut away to form tails in the back. It was close-fitting through the torso and had long cuffed sleeves, pockets, and a standing collar.

Redingote (RED-in-goat) — a fitted,

double-breasted man's coat adapted by the French from the English in the second half of the century. Some coats had two or three short capes added to form a carrick (see "Clothing Details: Coats").

Pantaloons — a variation of the sailor's trouser for men, adopted in the early 1790's. They had a buttoned fly, or flap front opening and first tied below the knee, then later reached the ankle. The patriots of the French Revolution wore them and became known as "sans-culottes," without breeches.

Incroyable, les incroyables — "the incredibles," the dandies of the eighteenth century, who wore an exaggerated version of English costume. With shaggy hair, and a coat that had a wide turnover collar, broad lapels and was rarely closed, incroyables had a somewhat sloppy appearance. Breeches stopped below the knees, and coat and vest often alternated between striped and solid-color fabric. A black collar on the coat signified aristocracy, a red, revolutionary. See Figure 3-12.

The tricorne hat remained popular during the eighteenth century, and was usually trimmed only with braid. The English Macaronies wore a small version of the tricorne on their wigs. A bicorne hat was popular from the reign of Louis XVI to the end of the century. Revolutionaries wore a soft, red cap with a hanging point trimmed with red, white, and blue cockade (knot of ribbon). Other wide-brimmed hats were worn, including the Quaker, with a low crown, and the Pennsylvania, with a flat crown. "Anglomania" at the end of the century resulted in the high crowned, or top hat.

Wigs remained popular through the century, although powdering died out. Wigs with pigtails in back were the most popular style. Other styles included the bagwig, which had a bag enclosing the tail; the cadogan, which had a tie around the tail and neck; and the hedgehog, which had a bristly crown instead of rolled hair.

Coats for men were double-breasted with high turnover collars, lapels, long sleeves, and cutaway tailoring. The waistcoat of the late years of the century was sleeveless, often double-breasted, cut square at the waist, and had lapels.

Lightweight boots were worn all century. So were *spatterdashes* (leather leggings) and *gaiters* (linen leggings that buttoned onto the calf).

Contouche (con-TOOSH) — a loose gown with back box pleats, worn over a tight bodice and an underskirt at the beginning of the century.

Watteau (wa-TOE) — a gown worn by women during the Regency, named after the painter Jean Antoine Watteau. The pleated back flowed from the shoulders. The front sometimes hung loose, or it was fitted at the waist. The sleeves were usually to the elbow, and the neck was cut low. See Figure 3-11.

Robe à la Française — a version of the Watteau popular by the 1730's. Six stitched box pleats in back opened into a train, and the bodice was tight. The robe was worn over an underskirt with panniers.

Panniers — the wide hoop shape that had returned to popularity by the 1730's (see "Seventeenth Century"). It grew to exaggerated proportions at the sides with flat front and back. The hoop itself rarely reached below the hips. Pocket panniers had holes through which the skirt could be pulled and were usually styled with a Watteau back. Elbow panniers were so wide that the wearer could rest her elbows on them. See Figure 3-11.

Mlle. Rose Bertin — the dressmaker for Marie Antoinette. Dolls dressed with her

Outline of Costume History

court fashions were sent to major cities as a gesture of goodwill.

Polonaise — a gown worn by women during the reign of Marie Antoinette. It had three panniers, one on each side and one in back, that were gathered on cords. It was ornamented with tassels and rosettes. See Figure 3-11.

Tourneur — a crinoline bustle that replaced the panniers hoop by the mid-

Figure 3-11. Eighteenth Century Costumes.

1720's: Watteau

Late 1790's: French Incroyable

1780's. The polonaise could be worn over it.

Queen's Gown — a lightweight cotton or silk gown popularized by Marie Antoinette. It had a deep neckline, a ruffle collar and hem, and a wide sash at the waist.

Merveilleuse (mare-vay-OOZ) — the female equivalent of the Directoire's incroyable. The gowns were high waisted with a low neckline and were made from transparent, clingy fabrics. They were worn over a light slip or flesh-colored tights. Very often they were modeled after the draped garments of the classical Greek and Roman periods. Long, sheer scarves were wrapped around the neck. See Figure 3-12.

The French Revolution saw women wear gowns with higher waists, gathered skirts over petticoats, tight bodices, and white fichus (see "Clothing Details: Collars"). High-heeled slippers gave way to ballet slippers and finally to sandals for the Merveilleuse.

Accessories included silk and leather gloves, large muffs, aprons, fans, corsages, scarves, watch fobs, parasols, canes, cameos, and miniatures. Elaborate hair styles requiring a hairdresser or wigs were worn throughout the century, including the Revolution. Caps to cover these hair styles were worn. During the reign of Marie Antoinette hats of all sizes, shapes, and materials became popular, especially hats with very wide brims with lots of decoration. Bonnets and decorated high crowned hats were worn during the Revolution. The Merveilleuse often wore bonnets with large front brims.

Nineteenth Century

Breeches and Trousers — during the French Empire through 1830 breeches and trousers were snug-fitting and were made from stretchy fabrics, especially knit stockinette, buckskin, and nankeen. The trousers that gained greatest acceptance were ankle length and had a strap that went under the boot. These lasted until the 1850's, then trouser legs became wider. Button fly front closings were used on most trousers by 1850. Front and back creases in trousers were accepted by the 1890's.

Waistcoats — waistcoats made of pique were worn during the French Empire. They became more tightly fitted, and waistlines were cut smaller in the 1880's. Decorative fabrics were used for formal waistcoats, and white waistcoats were popular in the second half of the century.

Greatcoats — a fitted, double-breasted redingote and a double-breasted carrick were worn through 1830. Knee-length redingotes that were single- or double-breasted first appeared in the second decade and continued through the fourth decade. See Figure 3-13.

Frock Coat with Claw-Hammer Tails — a man's overcoat with split tails in back, worn only in daytime in the first two decades of the century, then, in the second half of the century, worn only for formal attire.

Box Coat — a short, square, man's topcoat, single- or double-breasted with a shawl collar. The box coat first appeared in the late 1830's.

Sack Coat — a single- or double-breasted jacket that had no waistline seam. It was the important jacket with trousers in the second half of the century. Tuxedo was the formal sack coat of the 1800's. See Figure 3-13.

Prince Albert Coat — a double-breasted frock coat worn in the second half of the century.

Cravats — were worn throughout the century. At the beginning of the century

Outline of Costume History   **65**

two cravats were often combined. Beau Brummel, the epitome of dandyism, was renowned for his ability to tie a cravat. Mufflers were also wrapped around the neck and tied as were neckcloths, which were often held in place by stickpins. Bow ties were worn for formal occasions. Ascots were popular in England in the later decades of the century (see "Clothing Details: Necklines").

Figure 3-12. Eighteenth Century Costumes.

1770's: Polonaise with Panniers   *Late 1790's: French Merveilleuse*

Lingerie Gowns — the sheer gowns of the Directoire period carried over into the French Empire with the addition of long puffed sleeves and a small ruff. Empress Josephine of the First French Empire changed this gown to one with a high waist, short, puffed sleeves, a square decolletage, and a train. A more elaborate version had long, tight sleeves and a train hanging from the left shoulder. See Figure 3-14.

Canezou (can-ZOO) — a short, tight,

Figure 3-13. Nineteenth Century Costumes.

Top Hat

Bowler or Derby Hat

1840's: Redingote and Trousers.

1870's: Sack Coat and Contrasting Trousers.

Outline of Costume History

sleeveless vest that pulled on over the head and was worn through the 1840's. It was often lacy or transparent.

Spencer — a short, snug bolero jacket with long sleeves, worn by women with Empire-styled gowns.

Gabriel — a long, princess-styled dress (see "Clothing Details: Dresses"), first introduced in the 1860's.

Shawls — square or triangular wraps first made popular in Europe by the Empress Josephine, worn throughout this century. They were usually large and often of luxurious fabrics.

Corsets — returned in the 1820's and cinched the natural waist. A bell-shaped, ankle-length skirt with all types of trim was worn with a bodice that had long full

Figure 3-14. Nineteenth Century Costumes.

Early 1800's: Empire

1850's: Crinoline

sleeves and bertha collars. The leg-o'-mutton sleeve was popular. This style lasted through the 1830's.

Crinoline — a horsehair underskirt that replaced the layers of petticoats worn until the early 1840's. A decade later the crinoline became a bell-shaped cage hoop, worn under a tight-bodiced gown with a high neck for day and a low neck for evening. By the mid-1860's, the bell-shaped hoop became more conical. During the American Civil War, hoop skirts became very full, accenting tight bodices. The crinoline decreased in size toward the end of the 1860's, and a pointed peplum (see "Clothing Details: Dresses") was added over the skirt. The crinoline era ended with the 1860's. See Figure 3-14.

Bustle — an exaggerated fullness at the back of the skirt. The bustle returned to popularity at the end of the 1860's (replacing the crinoline) and was the major fashion of the 1870's. The bustle skirt with a train was slimmed down with a peplum at the end of the 1870's, but the bustle returned again in the 1880's under a skirt topped with a tight-fitting bodice that formed a point below the waist. The bustle was out of fashion by the 1890's. See Figure 3-15.

Woman's Suit — a tailored skirt, jacket, and shirt combination that first appeared in the 1860's. It became popular at the end of the 1880's and has remained in fashion.

Gibson Girl Look — the hourglass silhouette of the 1890's ("Gay Nineties") having a curved bodice starting wide at the shoulders and coming in slim at the waist to a narrow-hipped, bell-shaped skirt with a train. The bodice often had soft folds that overlapped the waistline. See Figure 3-15.

Sport Clothes — outfits designed for women's participation in many sports of the 1890's such as bicycling, tennis, and sailing.

Redingotes — long, double-breasted women's coats with capes worn during the first three decades of the century. Fur was added in the 1830's, turning the redingote into a *pelisse,* but the redingote without capes or fur returned in the 1890's.

Furs — fur capes or *tippets* were popular for women in the 1830's. Fur coats were important during the 1870's and 1880's.

Hats — men wore narrow-brimmed top hats throughout the century. Felt or straw hats with rolled brims and low crowns were worn for sport in the second half of the century. The bowler or derby appeared in the 1850's and the homburg or fedora in the last two decades of the century. See Figure 3-13. Women wore turbans through the 1830's, and bonnets and caps through the 1860's. Brimmed hats with streamers appeared in the 1820's, and the "porkpie hat" was popular. Bonnets returned in the 1870's and 1880's. They were extravagantly decorated with ribbons, veils, flowers, or feathers, and were worn pushed back from the forehead to the top of the head. In the 1890's, heavily ornamented toques (see "Renaissance") and brimmed hats were also worn right on the top of the head. See Figure 3-15.

Shoes — men wore boots under their trousers and breeches through the 1860's. *Wellingtons* and *Hessians* were the most popular styles. In the 1850's, a short, laced shoe appeared, but it was replaced in the 1860's with a side-buttoned style. Gaiters appeared in the 1870's and a buttoned, cloth-top shoe at the end of the century. See Figure 3-13. Men wore socks under their shoes and boots. Women wore ballet-type slippers through the first half of the century.

Outline of Costume History

Pointed-toe shoes with soles, high heels, and buttoned or laced soft tops were worn from the 1860's through the 1880's. Heeled slippers were originally worn only at night, until the last decade of the century. High buttoned boots also appeared in the 1890's.

Accessories — fans, handkerchiefs, gloves, and parasols were popular through the 1870's and again in the 1890's. Hair ornaments were worn through the 1830's and were worn for evening in the 1860's and 1880's. Lockets, cameos, watches, and chains were popular at the beginning of the century and again in the 1850's and 1860's. Colored stockings were worn in the latter half of the century. In the 1890's stock-

Figure 3-15. Nineteenth Century Costumes.

1880's: Bustle

1890's: Gay Nineties

ings were black and often had lacy patterns.

Twentieth Century

The sack coat and trousers of the nineteenth century carried over as the basic dress for men of the twentieth century.

Men's Suit Jackets — had broad, padded shoulders in the first decade of the century. By 1910 the padding was removed and the "natural shoulder" look began. During the years of World War I, the jacket became more fitted through the high waist and was fastened with one button. The twenties saw the jacket become less fitted and adorned with patch pockets and a two-button closing. The "English drape" jacket came in at the end of the twenties and lasted through most of the thirties. It had one button and was very loose over the chest. At the end of the decade, the jacket returned to the higher, front-closing, two-button jacket. World War II and the forties saw three-button single- and double-breasted jackets with a truly natural shoulder. Contrasting sport jackets were acceptable at this time.

Trousers — became much fuller at the beginning of the century than those worn at the end of the nineteenth century. Knickerbockers (knickers) were worn for sports. Leather belts also became popular. In the twenties, trousers and knickers became fuller. "Oxford bags," the fullest trousers, measured up to 24 inches at the hems. "Plus fours" is a term describing knickers that fell to four inches below the knee. White summer slacks became popular in the twenties. Pleats at the waistline were added to the already baggy trousers of the thirties. In the forties, trousers had pressed pleats and were often worn in colors contrasting the jacket.

Coats — men's polo coats (see "Clothing Details: Coats") became popular at the beginning of the century and went on to become a classic style. The raccoon coat was the sporty fur coat of the twenties. The trench coat evolved from the soldier's coat of World War I. Many nineteenth century overcoat styles moved into the twentieth century, but the Chesterfield became the favorite (see "Clothing Details: Coats").

Shirts — men's knit sports shirts like the basque and the polo (see "Clothing Details: Shirts") gained lasting popularity from the beginning of the century. In the twenties a soft, detachable shirt collar for dress shirts appeared, and by the thirties it was permanently attached to shirts. This collar was often held in place by a bar pin that connected the points but was hidden by the necktie. White shirts remained popular for daytime and formal dress through the forties. Dark-colored sport shirts were seen in the thirties. The forties' sport shirt was also colored and had a convertible collar (see "Clothing Details: Collars").

Gibson Girl — this look, created in the 1890's, carried over into the first decade of the twentieth century. A corset threw the bust forward and the hips back, forming an S shape. The waistline was small, and evening dresses had low necklines. This look straightened out by the end of the first decade.

Hobble Skirt — a skirt of tubular shape that was popular after the S shape of the Gibson Girl went out of fashion. The skirt was named "hobble" because it was banded from the knee down, close to the leg, and thus women found it difficult to walk in it. The bodice over this skirt had an off-the-shoulder neckline and kimono sleeves (see "Clothing Details: Sleeves").

Outline of Costume History

Orientalism—the second decade craze that included the hobble skirt, harem pants under skirts, tunics over skirts, and a peg-top skirt that was draped over the hips, becoming narrower below. See Figure 3-16.

The Flapper—an era in which the total look was straight without the curves of waist or bust. See Figure 3-16. By 1925 skirts were raised to the knee. Although many thought the length scandalous, skirts were raised above the knee in 1927. Skirts, blouses, and sweaters were seen during this era and continued after it.

Figure 3-16. Twentieth Century Costumes.

1914: Kimono Sleeve Jacket, Peg-Top Skirt

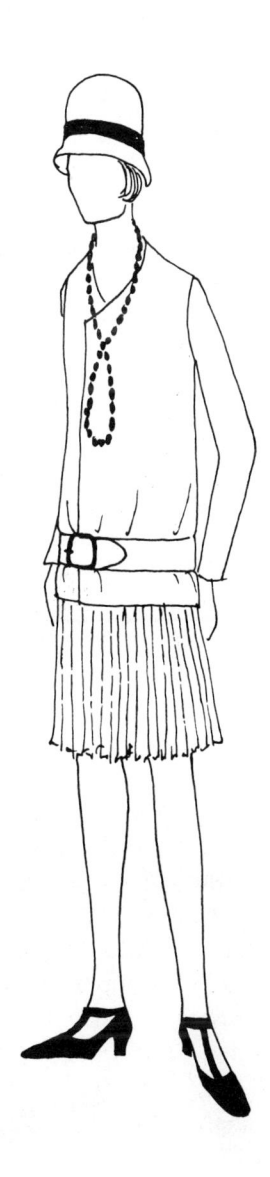

1920's: Flapper

The Thirties — in this period, skirt lengths descended to 10 inches above the floor for daytime and to the floor for evening. The waistline returned to normal and the bustline was again empha- sized. Outfits designed for special occasions flourished. Clothing was made for every function or sport. Wide, padded shoulders (see Figure 3-17), halter necklines, bare midriffs, and the return of

---

Figure 3-17. Twentieth Century Costumes.

1930's: Padded Shoulder Suit

1947: New Look

the shirtwaist were all important. Pants appeared at this time and continued in popularity.

World War II — the thirties fashions continued, but colors and fabrics were subdued. There was little opportunity or desire for change, although skirts did get shorter. Pants were worn in the factories, and the jumpsuit became popular.

"The New Look" — new fabrics became available after World War II, and designers began to create women's clothes that were radically changed from the slim, straight, twentieth century silhouette. The French haute couture designer Christian Dior fathered a collection known as "The New Look" that was in a short time seen in Europe and America. Shoulders were natural, the bosom round, the waist cinched tight, the skirt very full over layers of petticoats, and the hemline dropped to mid-calf. See Figure 3-17.

Shoes — men wore high-laced or buttoned shoes for the first three decades. The low-laced shoe, the oxford, was worn from the beginning of the century until it eventually replaced the high-laced one. Men's sport shoes, those in white buckskin or saddle combinations for example, gained popularity in the twenties. The loafer was the sport shoe of the forties and was adapted to wear with suits. Women's oxfords, slippers, and pumps replaced the high-laced or buttoned shoe by the end of the first decade. Slippers and pumps continued through World War II. Spike heels arrived in the thirties.

Hosiery — black or brown stockings made of lisle or silk were popular for women in the first decade. The second decade saw the colors change to taupe, gray, or tan. Light- or flesh-colored stockings came in with the twenties and continued through World War II. Rayon and cotton or rayon lisle replaced silk for stockings. Nylon appeared briefly at the end of the thirties, but was withdrawn from consumer use for a period during the war. After World War II, sheer nylon stockings took over the hosiery market.

Hats — nineteenth century hats carried over into the twentieth, although men wore beret-type hats and visors and goggles for automobile driving at the beginning of the century. A slouch felt hat appeared in the twenties. Straw hats, usually with flat crowns and a brim, were worn in the summer. The overwhelming hats that women wore during the first decade gave way to the cloche, a small-brimmed, close-fitting hat, and the headache band, a ribbon worn around the forehead, of the twenties. Veils, caps, nets, and small, decorative hats were important through the thirties. See Figures 3-16 and 3-17.

Projects for Costume History

1. Study contemporary clothing. Research the changes in men's and/or women's clothing from 1947 to the present. Write and illustrate a report; use original drawings as well as clippings. Construct a Costume History Time Line and fill in the important events that have occurred since 1947.
2. Choose a period in history. Research it thoroughly and write a report on the mode of dress for the period. Include footnotes, a bibliography, and illustrations.
3. Read a novel, a play, or a biography and note references to costumes. Discuss how the costumes reflect the attitudes and values of the period. Examples of books:
   A. *My Life* by Isadora Duncan
   B. *Gone With the Wind*
   C. *The Great Gatsby*
   D. *The Importance of Being Earnest*
   E. *Anthony and Cleopatra*
   F. *My Fair Lady*
4. In science fiction novels and movies, the costumes of the future often have great significance. Choose three different science fiction works and compare the costumes. Include illustrations.

Bibliography

Davenport, Millia. ***The Book of Costume.*** New York: Crown Publishers, Inc., 1964.

Evans, Mary. ***Costume Throughout the Ages.*** Philadelphia: J. B. Lippincott Co., 1950.

Kohler, Carl, and Schardt, Emma Von. ***A History of Costume.*** New York: Dover Publications, Inc., 1963.

Laver, James. ***The Concise History of Costume and Fashion.*** New York: Charles Scribner's Sons, 1974.

Laver, James. ***Taste and Fashion.*** rev. ed. London: George A. Harrap & Co., Ltd., 1946.

Payne, Blanche. ***History of Costume: From the Ancient Egyptians to the Twentieth Century.*** New York: Harper & Row, 1965.

Roach, Mary Ellen, and Eicher, Joanne Bubolz, eds. ***Dress, Adornment, and the Social Order.*** New York: John Wiley & Sons, Inc., 1965.

Wilcox, R. Turner. ***The Dictionary of Costume.*** New York: Charles Scribner's Sons, 1963.

Wilcox, R. Turner. ***The Mode in Costume.*** New York: Charles Scribner's Sons, 1942.

4

National Costumes

Television, movies, newspapers, magazines, and travel quickly spread the news of the latest fashion trends. The national costumes of the world have, for the most part, been replaced by contemporary dress. Even in the countries that have retained their native dress, current styles are worn in the business and international communities. The farthest reaches of country, desert, or jungle are no longer immune to the changes of fashion.

This chapter deals with the national dress of many of the countries of the world. In some areas the costumes are still worn every day. In other areas the costumes are donned only for festivals or special occasions. Still in other areas the costumes have become a part of history.

Fashion designers use national costumes for style inspirations. Designers can study costumes by visiting special museum collections, such as the extensive Costume Institute of the Metropolitan Museum of Art in New York City. (The drawings in this chapter were done from costumes on display there.) Designers can learn about costume through books, period paintings, sculpture, or tapestries. They can be influenced by the costumes in movie or theater productions with historic or foreign themes. They can see national costumes firsthand on vacations and business trips to other countries.

A national costume, a Spanish flamenco dancer's, for example, might become the inspiration for a similar contemporary garment in a nontraditional fabric. Some manufacturers or retailers might import and sell native dress "as is." An example is embroidered Mexican peasant blouses. Traditional fabric, such as Indian sari cloth or Scottish tartans, might find new life in contemporary fashions. Accessories, such as the obi sash, might find their place on current apparel. Costumes from period movies such as *The Great Gatsby* might influence the look of clothes worn on the streets. A good designer will always be looking for style ideas, and they can be found in national costumes, a rich resource.

Certainly each country has many more items of apparel and more accessories than are mentioned here. Only the key items of a nation's costumes will be discussed. More detail about regions, countries, and people is available at libraries and museums. This is just an overview.

Europe

Current fashions are worn throughout Europe today. The peasant costumes of European countries are reserved almost entirely for festivals and special occasions. The women's costumes usually include long full skirts, blouses, and aprons. Headdresses are important. Embroidery is widely used as decoration.

England

The *smock* is the principal item of English national dress. It is a shirt with smocking detail on the yoke and cuffs. The color and fabric of the smock varied according to area, and it was worn by both men and women. See Figure 4-1.

Figure 4-1. English Smock.

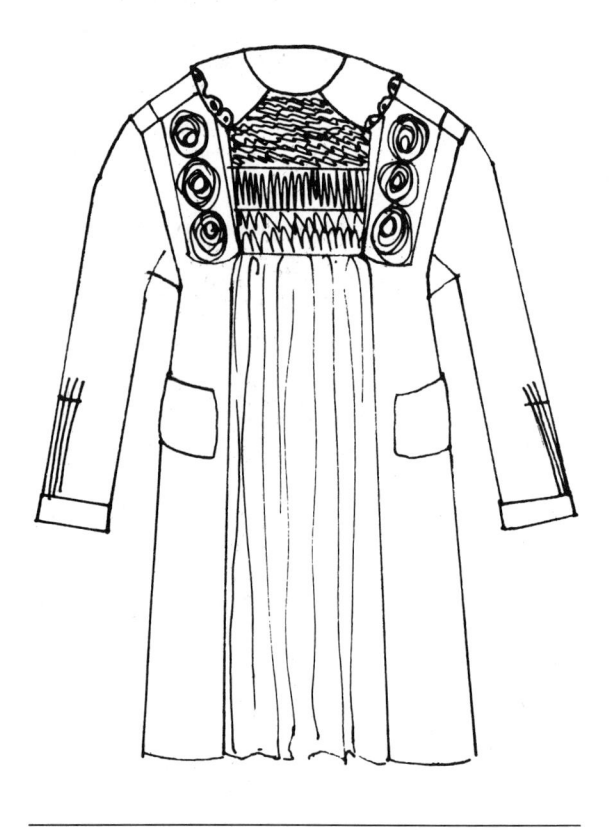

Scotland

The best known Scottish costume is the men's Highland attire. This includes a *kilt* or a short pleated skirt, shirt, short jacket, wool Highland bonnet, and *breacan-feile* or rectangular plaid shawl. The kilt and breacan-feile are both made of tartan plaid fabric. Each Scottish clan has a different tartan. The beautiful Paisley shawls also come from Scotland.

Denmark

Danish women wore long, embroidered skirts with pleated aprons. The embroidery designs were primarily of people, animals, birds, or flowers.

Norway

Norwegian women wore a pinafore with embroidered straps attached to the bodice. The pinafore was worn over a lingerie blouse. An interesting headdress that was worn is the *skaut,* a starched piece of white linen folded and fastened in the back. See Figure 4-2.

Sweden

Swedish women's long skirts had a colored border and were worn with an apron and a blouse with an embroidered collar and a laced-up bodice. See Figure 4-3. Men's shirts also had embroidery.

Finland

In Finland geometric patterns were used, especially in the favorite colors of the Finnish people — red and blue. A pleated wool jumper was worn by women. See Figure 4-4.

Lapland

(Lapland is not a separate country but is a region that spreads over northern Norway, Sweden, Finland, and the Soviet Union.) The traditional costume for Lapp men is a blue flannel tunic or *kapta,* cuffed and bordered with red; pointed boots made of reindeer skin; and a four-cornered *hat of the four winds,*

National Costumes

which can also serve as a purse or pillow. See Figure 4-5. The women's traditional attire is a long version of the men's tunic, plus a shawl and an embroidered earlap bonnet. Both men's and women's costumes include an anklet that can have pompons. In the winter months the Lapps traditionally wear furs.

The Netherlands

The best known Dutch garment is the starched, sheer lace and cotton cap with a pointed crown and turned up pointed sides. Other regional headdresses include the starched lace bonnet with wired wings from Zeeland. Men's costumes include full breeches, a short jacket, and a peaked cap.

See Figure 4-6. Traditional footwear for men and women includes wooden shoes called sabots.

Germany

Embroidery is the outstanding feature of German folk costumes. It appeared on full skirts worn over layers of petticoats, and combined with an apron, a corset, and a blouse. The blouse often had puffed sleeves and a lace bertha or shawl. The head covering was a scarf, or a felt or straw hat, the latter sometimes decorated with feathers or ribbons. Leather or cloth knee breeches with fancy stockings were the featured parts of the men's wardrobe.

Figure 4-2. Norwegian Costumes.

Little Norwegian Girl's Costume: Black wool pinafore with red edging and red, green, gold, and blue embroidery

Norwegian Tin Hat with Candle Holders

Norwegian Red Wool Hat with Navy, White, Green, and Brown Beads

Black Wool Norwegian Cap with Embroidered Flowers

Figure 4-3. Swedish Woman's Costume.

Figure 4-4. Finnish Navy and Red Wool Pleated Jumper.

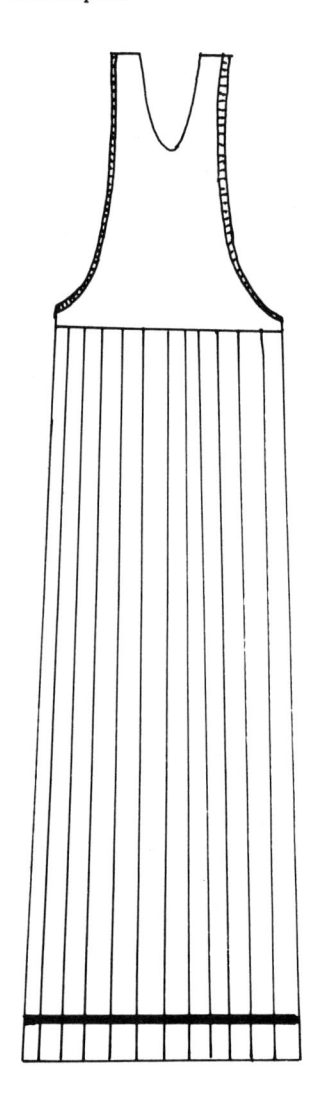

Flowered wool shawl; cream cotton blouse; red, black, and green corselette; blue cotton apron; black wool skirt with embroidery; black and silver embroidered bag; red wool hat with embroidery

Switzerland

Full skirts, aprons, full-sleeve blouses, and laced bodices were Swiss women's dress, as were elaborate headpieces including the *schlappe*, a black and white fan-shaped bonnet with ribbons and pleated wings. Men wore knee breeches, wool socks, a white shirt, a vest, a coat, and a skullcap or a felt brimmed hat.

Austria

The basic Austrian men's and women's costumes are similar to those of Germany and Switzerland. In the Tyrol of Austria embroidery was very important. Tyrolean men wore embroidered suspenders to hold up their leather or suede knee breeches. Sleeves on lace-trimmed blouses worn by Tyrolean women were unusually full and very ornate.

France

The typical French women's folk costume is comprised of a long full skirt, apron, separate bodice, and blouse. Shawls, many in printed fabrics, are often added to the costumes. Each region has a fancy woman's headdress distinguishing it from other regions. The largest headdresses come from Normandy and are usually starched lawn or muslin, are often pleated, and have lace trim. Large, stiff silk bows come from Alsace. White bonnets, sometimes topped with straw hats, come from southern France. Men's hats include felt or straw brimmed hats, fisherman's hats, top hats, berets, and tams. Trousers with a shirt, waistcoat, and jacket are other parts of the standard men's costume.

Spain

Parts of Spanish costume have international recognition today. One renowned part is the *mantilla,* a black or white lace head scarf worn over large, carved combs of tortoiseshell, ivory, or horn. The *manton de manilla* is a large, embroidered shawl with a deep fringe. Gypsy dancers of Spain still wear the traditional tiered and ruffled polka dot or checked gowns, an embroidered shawl, high-heeled

Figure 4-5. Man's Smock from Lapland.

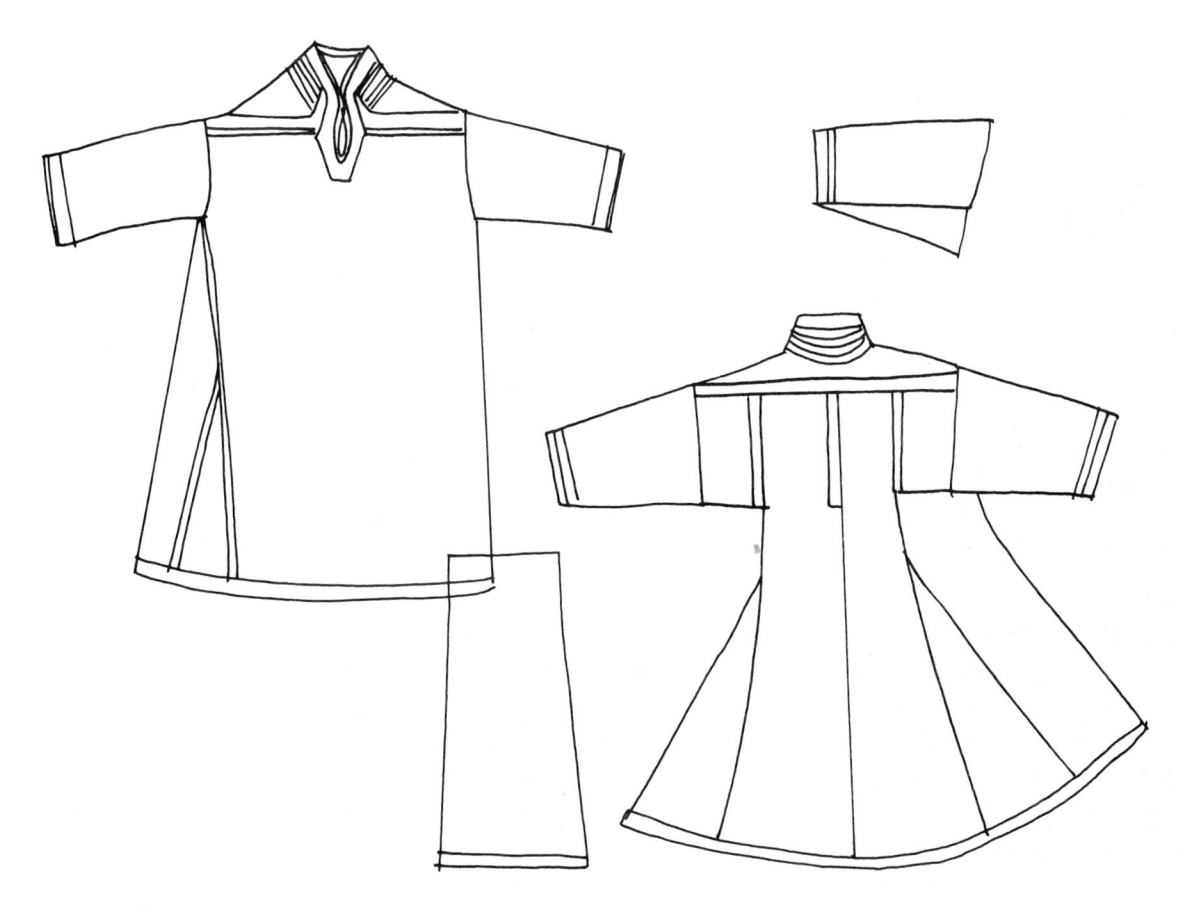

Figure 4-6. Dutchman's Wool Jacket.

slippers, and flowers in the hair. The torero's or bullfighter's costume also remains unchanged, combining gold or silver brocade with embroidery and velvet. It has tight, knee-length pants, a short bolero jacket, a

vest, a ruffled shirt, a thin tie, a cape, black stockings and slippers, and is topped by a heavy horned hat of black cloth with braid and ribbon. Figure 4-7 shows a Spanish jacket and vest.

Portugal

Portuguese women wore frilly blouses, shawls, kerchiefs, and skirts covered with elaborate aprons. The most unusual garment of Portugal is sheepskin leggings worn by shepherds.

Italy

The peasant costumes of Italy are very festive. For women, embroidery, ribbons, or lace trim the long skirt, and two aprons might be layered over the skirt. The bodice is often patterned, and the blouse has intricate neck and

Figure 4-7. Spanish Costumes.

Sleeveless Heavy Black Wool Jacket with Silver Buttons from Segovia Spain

Spaniard's Black Pile Jacket

National Costumes

sleeve detail, and sometimes unusual oversleeves. The range of head coverings extends from the simple kerchief to elaborate headdresses. Men's hats can be round or cone shaped, felt or straw, flower or ribbon trimmed. In Sardinia, a knitted, stockinglike cap is worn by men that also serves as a kind of purse.

Greece

Eastern influence is apparent in Greek costumes. Although Turkish style pantaloons and tunics have been worn by Greek men, it is the costume of the *evzone*, the select infantryman, that is remembered. The costume consists of a pleated, white linen kilt called a *fustenella*, a shirt, and a slashed sleeve bolero that has cording trim. A *phrygian* cap with a tassel (a pointed, soft, hoodlike cap), stockings, and sometimes garters or pompoms are also parts of the costume. The fustenella was adapted to other Greek costumes. Women's costume consists of tunics over blouses and skirts, sleeveless vests detailed with braid and embroidery, aprons, and kerchiefs as head coverings. See Figure 4-8.

Yugoslavia

Each area of Yugoslavia has a costume that is distinctive and identifies the people of the area. In Macedonia the women's tunic, skirt, vest, apron, and head scarf can be heavily decorated with embroidery, braid, lace, ribbon, beads, or coins. Macedonian men's costume has a white tunic and breeches, a vest, a sleeveless, braid-trimmed coat, and a fez (a brimless hat that is usually red with a black or blue tassel, originally from Turkey). The vest and apron of the women in Serbia are embroidered, and the blouses are trimmed in white lace. In Bosnia and Montenegro, men's wear includes Turkish style breeches, sashed shirt or tunic, and braided or embroidered bolero. In Montenegro the men wear a *kapa*, a fezlike cap, with a block border.

Figure 4-8. Robe from Corinth, Greece.

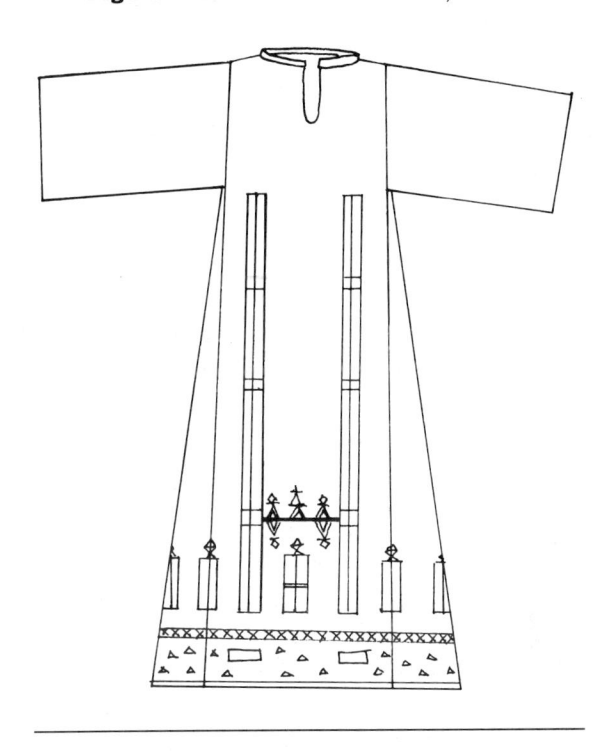

Bulgaria

The best known Bulgarian garment is the *jube*, which is a padded, sheepskin coat, made skin side out, and decorated with appliques and embroidery. It is worn by both men and women during the Balkan winters.

Albania

White embroidered shirts and blouses with sashes, boleros and aprons were Albanian women's apparel. Men adapted the Middle Eastern *chalwar* (pantaloons) and the Greek *fustenella*, and wore them with a shirt, cummerbund, bolero, and tarboosh (brimless, felt cap with a tassel).

Hungary

Embroidery was very important in the clothing of Hungarian peasants. Aprons covered full skirts that were worn over layers of petticoats.

The *gatyák* were men's wide pantaloons sometimes having lace trim. The *szür* was a great felt or leather men's cloak in black or white with bold embroidery or appliques. Figure 4-9 shows a Hungarian man's sheepskin coat.

Rumania

Rumanian men and women wore a short, embroidered sheepskin vest trimmed with lamb's wool as part of their costume. Men also wore a long coat version over their smocks and breeches.

Poland

A variation of Rumania's sheepskin vest was worn by Polish men and women. The sleeveless vest or coat has the skin side out, fur edging, embroidery, and appliques.

Soviet Union

The Soviet Union covers a wide area stretching across Eurasia from the Baltic Sea to the Bering Sea and includes many different peoples with a variety of customs. Today drab, modern dress is common throughout the country, especially in the major cities and industrial areas.

Women's dress in western Russia (including the area on the Baltic Sea, the Ukraine, the Caucasus, and the lands around the Volga), is based upon peasant garb, a skirt and blouse combination with heavy (usually red) embroidery. See Figure 4-10. The *paneva,* a long, checked wool skirt, was commonly worn. Long band-neck shirts with embroidery at the neck, sleeves, and hem were sometimes worn belted as a dress. Skirts were also worn under a *sarafan* or jumperlike dress often worn for festivals. Fancy aprons, bodices, head scarves, or embroidered caps completed the attire. Men also wore embroidery on their shirts or tunics that were

Figure 4-9. Hungarian Man's Sheepskin Coat.

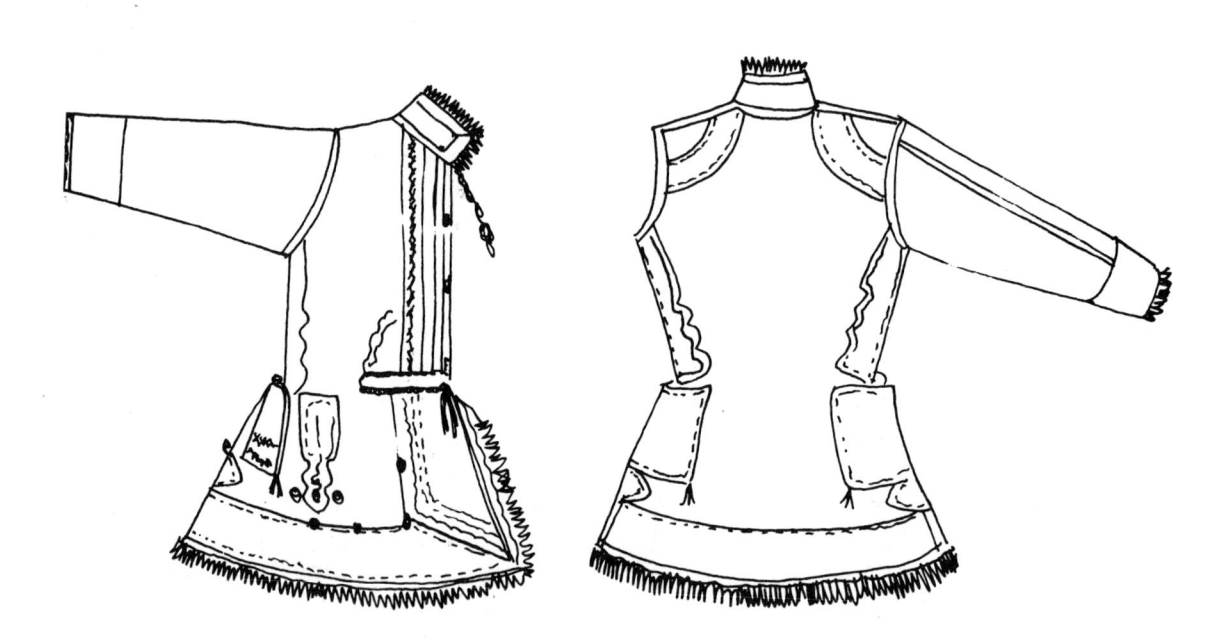

National Costumes

worn over baggy trousers. The trousers were often tucked into boots. Cossack and Georgian men topped their shirts and trousers with a short or long wrap coat with bullet pouches across the chest. Multishaped hats of karakul lamb completed the outfit. See Figure 4-11.

Turkish costume influenced the dress in the central Asian sectors of the Soviet Union. Men and women dressed similarly, both wearing a *caftan* (a loose robe with an open front and wide sleeves) or dolman (a cloak with sleeves) over a blouse, and trousers that tucked into boots. See Figure 4-12. Hats included large ones of sheepskin and variations on the *kola,* a stiff, small, brimless hat. Color, prints, and embroidery were all important.

The traditional garb in Siberia, hardly seen today, consists of boots with pants, a knee-length hair or fur shirt, a fur collar, and a hat or hood. A decorative chest piece distinguished the various groups in this harsh nothern region. The *del,* a robe that overlaps to a double thickness in front, was the outer garment worn in eastern central Asia including parts of Mongolia, Manchuria, and Siberia.

Turkey

The Turkish influence in dress can be seen throughout the Balkans and the Caucasus. Men and women wore variations of the Middle Eastern *chalwar* (full pantaloons), and

Figure 4-10. Russian and Moravian Costumes.

Embroidered Black Skirt and Embroidered Natural Cotton Blouse from Moravia (Czechoslovakia)

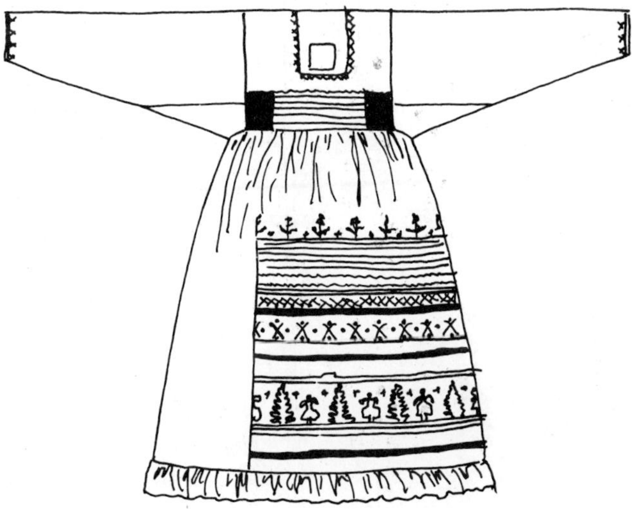

Embroidered Pleated and Shirred Woman's Dress in linen with navy and red from Tula in central Russia

added the *entari*, a blouse. Sometimes a bolero or a caftan was added. Men's costume included a fez (brimless hat, usually red with a black or blue tassel), and women's, a veil or *yashmak* to cover their faces in public.

The Middle East

Countries included under the heading Middle East are the Asian countries of Saudi Arabia, Jordan, Lebanon, Iraq, Syria, Kuwait, the United Arab Emirates, Qatar, Yemen, and Israel, plus the African nation of Egypt. The Israelis wear contemporary American or European dress. Moslem businessmen in the Arab countries have primarily adopted Western dress, but they often add to it their historic costumes. Some Moslem women, particularly those living in Egypt and those living elsewhere who work outside the home, have given up the traditional garments. The following are the principal items of traditional Middle Eastern costume.

Gandoura—a long, flowing robe worn by Moslem women that is also worn by men in Saudi Arabia and Egypt, sometimes in a short version.
Haik—a full-length cloth covering a woman from head to toe, worn in Saudi Arabia.
Yashmak—a women's face veil that exposes just the eyes. It can be worn with a

Figure 4-11. Russian Man's Costume.

Lesghian Jacket (Archaluk or Beshmet) from Kubátshi; high black leather boots; "papache" cap, all from South Eastern Caucasus

National Costumes

Figure 4-12. Russian Peasant Caftan in Cream with Red Stripes, Green Edging, and Navy Beads.

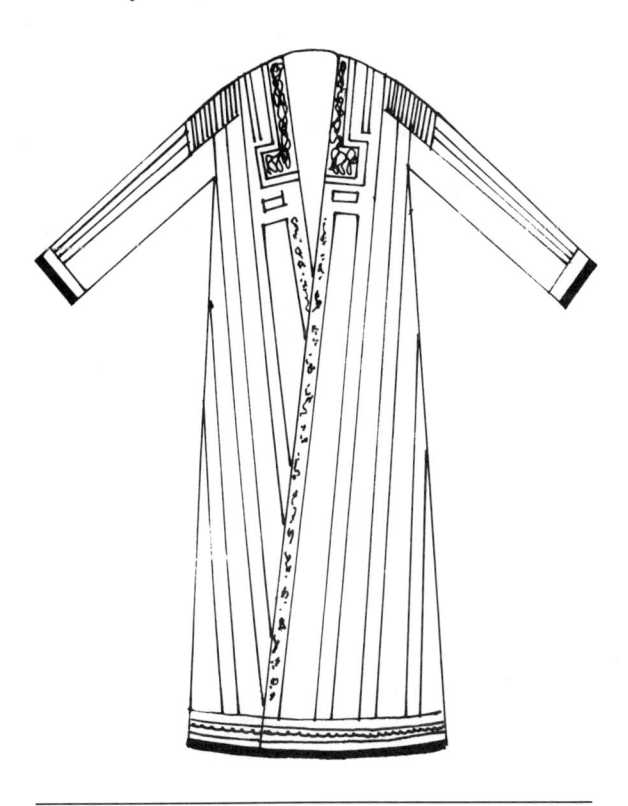

tarboosh, a *shatweh* (tall, conical hat), or a coin-decorated hat.

Mandeel — a face veil.

Barracan — a cloth wrapped around the body and over the head, worn by Palestinian women.

Tobe — a long white shirt worn under other robes by both men and women.

Chalwar — full pantaloons worn by women in Iraq and Yemen. Chalwar have been adapted by men and women of other countries.

Khurkeh — a long straight dress with a sash, embroidery on the bodice side slits, and a short bolero, worn by Palestinian women.

Kamis — a men's long-sleeve cotton shirt that can be worn long with a sash.

Kibr — a slim robe worn over the tobe.

Caftan — a long robe that overlaps in front, has long, full sleeves, and is often worn with a sash.

Aba — a loose, full cloak worn by Moslem men over their other apparel.

Kaffiyeh — a headcloth that is the standard head covering of Middle Eastern Arab men. The *agal*, a band of two cords often decorated with hair tufts or gold or silver threads, holds the kaffiyeh on the head.

Iran

Iran is the modern country evolved from the ancient kingdom of Persia. Today Western dress is seen in the cities and in the business community. The traditional men's costume combines trousers, a long sashed shirt, and a cloak. See Figure 4-13. The *kola* (a stiff, small, brimless hat) was also worn. Although women have worn western dress in past periods, there has been a return to the traditional dress, which includes the *chalwar* and *chadar* (a head to toe cloak).

Afghanistan

Afghanistan has been influenced by Iran as well as by central Asia and the subcontinent of India. Traditional men's costume includes full, wrapped pantaloons called *tombans,* a shirt or tunic that can be pleated, a vest, a kola or a turban, and a sheepskin cloak with the wool on the inside. Women are giving up purdah (the Moslem custom of veiling), but the typical dress is still the chalwar, the chadar, or the *burka* (a pleated, head-to-toe cloak), and embroidered vests. See Figure 4-14.

India and Pakistan

The costumes of India and Pakistan are basically similar, although Pakistani costume

88   Fashion: Color, Line, and Design

has had more influence from Persia. Women's national dress in Pakistan is an embroidered, mirror-decorated pants and tunic outfit called a *shalwa-kamis,* with a head scarf or *dupatta.* The *sari* is the most common women's garb in India. It is a piece of fabric, anywhere from six to ten yards long, which is wrapped, pleated, and draped around a woman's body, with one end left free to cover the head. It can be made of simple cotton cloth or of richer fabrics, including silk with gold or silver yarns. Under the sari is a short blouse, the *choli,* and a drawstring waist petticoat.

Costume for Indian village men is a cloth wrapped around the waist that is often pulled between the legs to form a loincloth. This is

Figure 4-13. Persian Costumes.

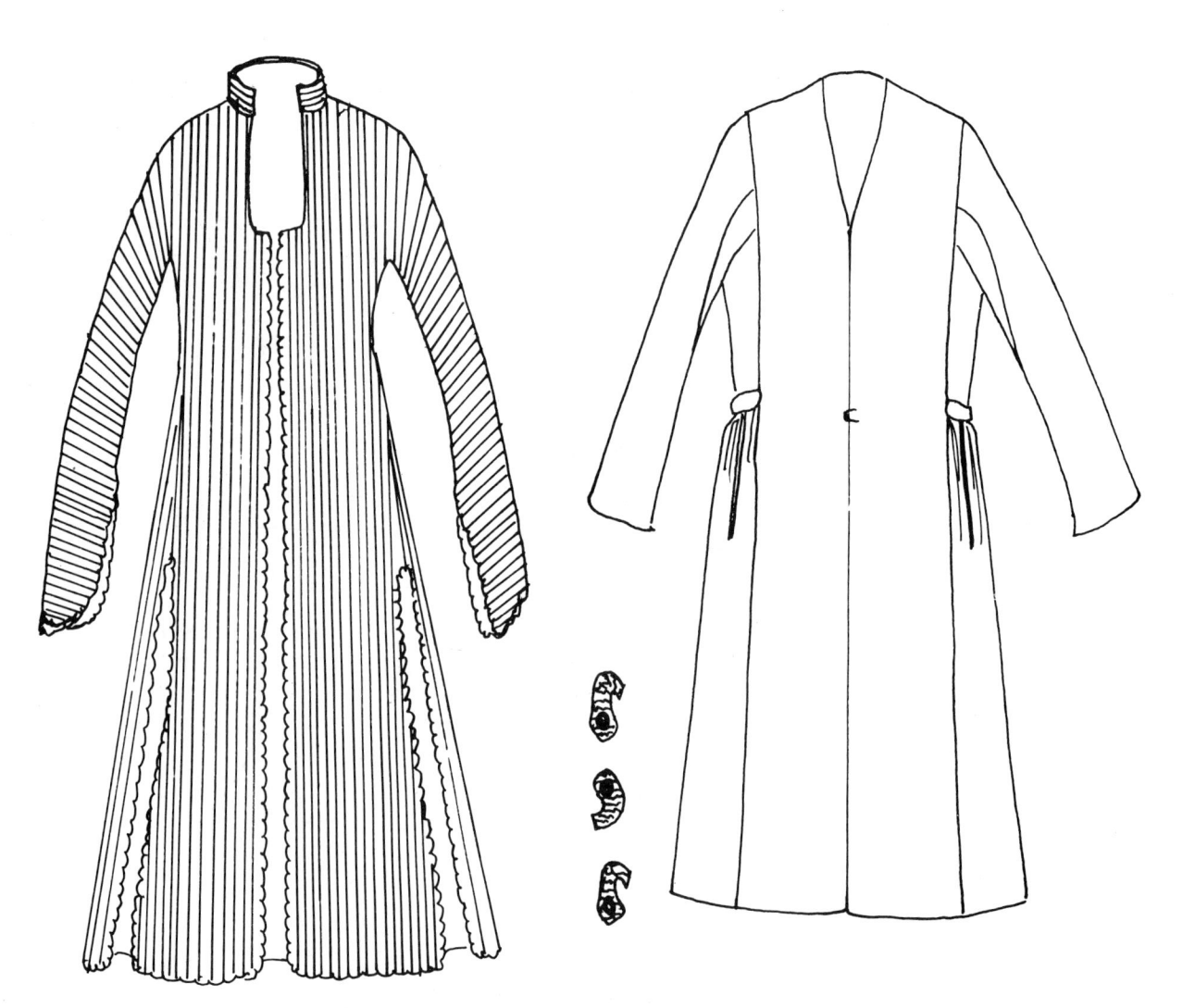

Persian Silk Coat with Orange, Violet, Beige, Blue, and Green Stripes

Persian Coat with Navy Ground and White, Violet, and Navy Pattern, Shown at Left

National Costumes

the *dhoti,* and it can be topped with a loose shirt. Costume of urban men in the north is a trouser and shirt combination, with Pakistanis wearing a kola and Indians a Gandhi cap. A single-breasted, stand-collar, side-vented coat, the *choga,* can be worn by men over jodhpurs and a collarless shirt, the *kurta.* A commonly seen head covering is the *pagri,* a wrapped turban.

The Himalaya Mountain Region consists of Kashmir, Tibet, Nepal, Bhutan, and Sikkim. There is much variety in costume in this region. Saris and dhotis are worn in Kashmir and Nepal. The loose, overlapping robe called the *chupa* is worn by Tibetan men and women. In some areas women wear it, adding an apron. The simplicity or ornamentation of the chupa's fabric reveals the status of the wearer. A wrapped, sashed and bloused robe with sleeves is popular for men throughout the region, and a wrap skirt or robe, a long-sleeved blouse, and a jacket are popular for the women. Scarves are important, with color and style signifying a person's rank in society. A variety of hat styles exists. See Figure 4-15.

Southeast Asia

A peaked straw hat is common throughout Southeast Asia, but other parts of the tradi-

Figure 4-14. Turkestan Woman's Overcoat of Red Velvet with Silver Threads. (Turkestan is a central Asian region overlapping the USSR, Afganistan and the Sinkiang Province of the People's Republic of China.)

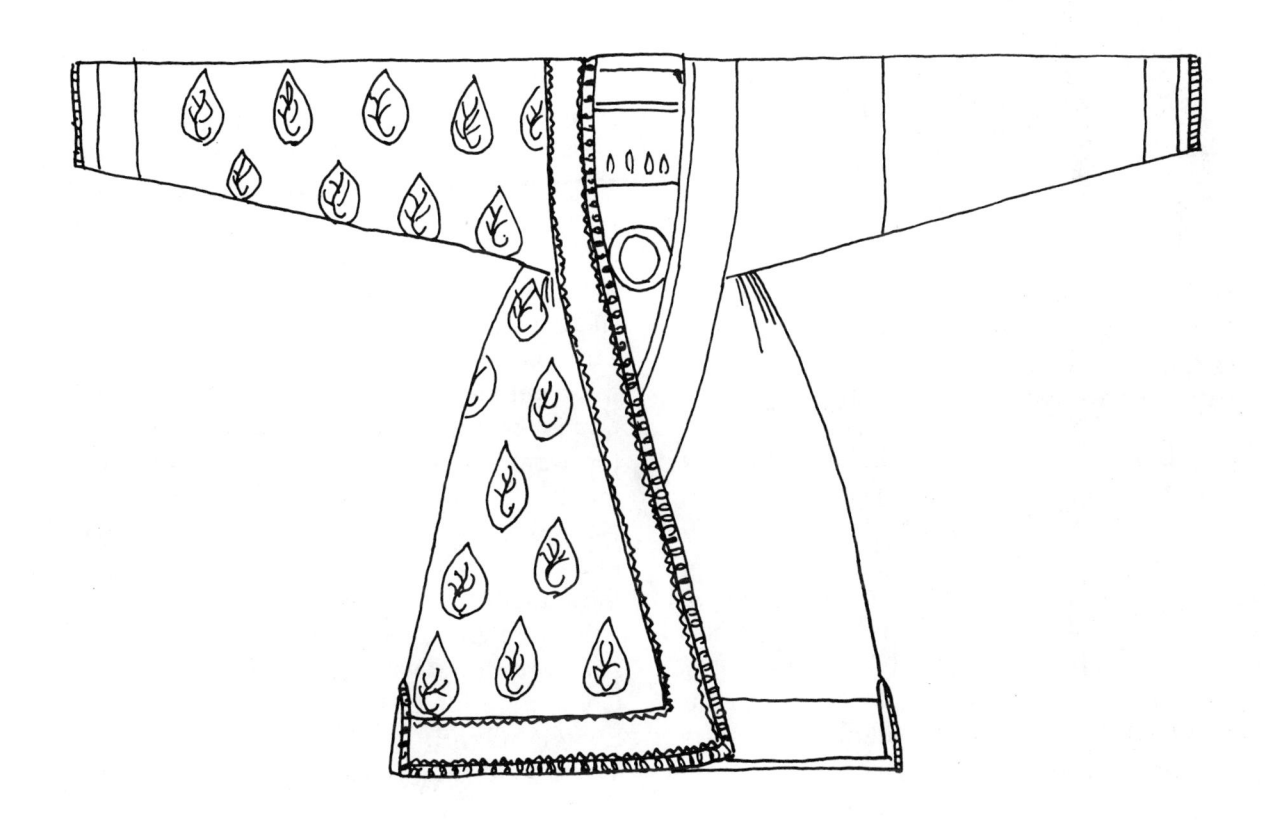

Figure 4-15. East Indian Cotton Coat Stitched for Quilted Effect with Flower Pattern in Each Box.

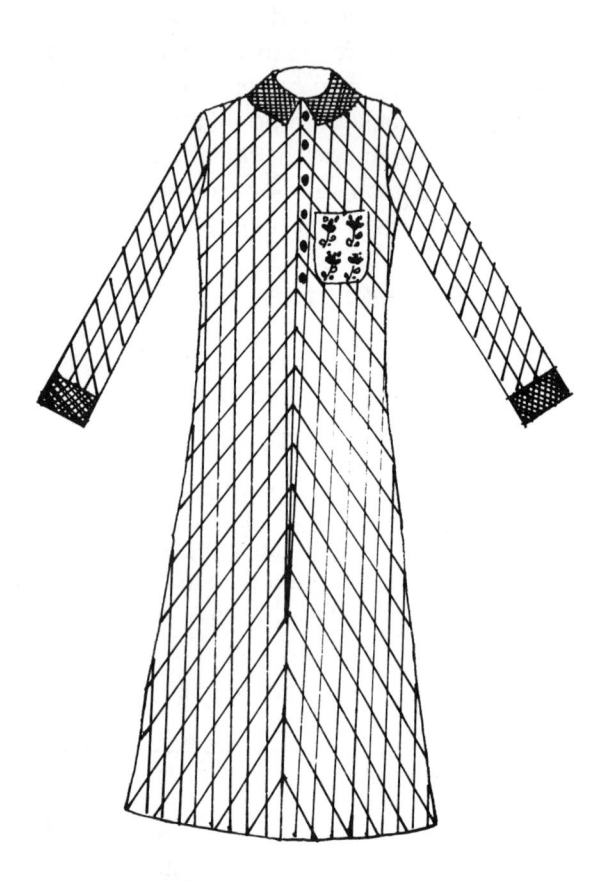

tional costume vary according to area. Men's clothing has become noticeably Westernized in recent years, whereas women's clothing has remained traditional. The following terms, highlight the costume of Southeast Asia.

Lungi — a saronglike skirt or dress worn by men and women of Burma.

Sampot — a dhotilike garment worn by women of Cambodia.

Panung — a wrapped skirt that can be worn like a dhoti. It is part of the traditional dress of Thailand.

Sinhs — a wraparound skirt worn by women of Laos. The men's costume is sampot.

Aodai — a sheer, slim chemise worn over pants or a skirt. It is the costume for women of Viet Nam.

Sarong — a long, wrapped skirt with front pleats. It is worn with the *kabaya* as the traditional costume of women in Indonesia.

Kabaya — long-sleeved jacket worn with a sarong as traditional costume of women in Indonesia.

Cheongsam — a high-collar, slim sheath with side slits, worn with the sarong and the sari as the traditional costume of women in Malaysia.

People's Republic of China

Dress today in the People's Republic of China is Spartan. Basically all men and women wear trousers and a jacket. Blue, gray, and brown are the standard colors. But China has a history of rich costumes. The traditional worker's costume paired a stand-collar jacket, which buttoned in the front or from side to back, with trousers or dhotilike pants. Hats included the skullcap, felt fedora, and brimmed, peaked straw hat. See Figure 4-16. A long slim robe with a stand collar, side to back closing, and side slits was worn with a short, sleeveless, stand-collar jacket that closed with buttons and loops. Wealthier Chinese had these garments made of silk in different colors and fabric designs and often had them quilted for warmth. See Figure 4-16. The *cheongsam*, the slim, stand-collar sheath with side slits of eight to ten inches, came from southern China but became the established women's wear throughout China. It was often in silk printed with flora or fauna. Slippers or clogs were standard footwear. The most extravagant Chinese costumes were the *dragon robes* of the eighteenth and nineteenth centuries. These were long, full silk robes for royalty and

National Costumes

nobility that were adopted as the dress of people of less prestige. At their most elaborate for the emperors, the dragon robes were embroidered and appliqued with many symbols,

Figure 4-16. Chinese Costumes.

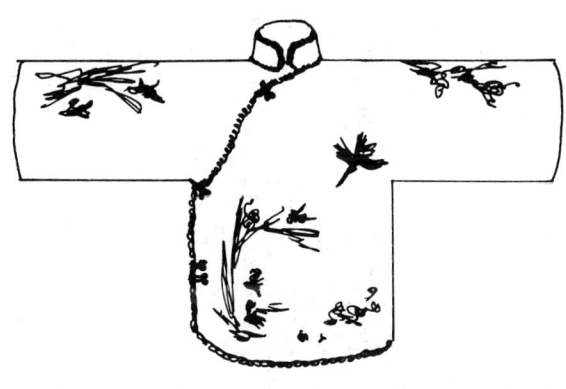

Chinese Jacket of Aqua Silk with Braid and Black, White, and Gray Embroidery

Chinese Silk Vest of Pale Blue with Gold, Salmon, and Blue Embroidery

Chinese Black Silk Cap with Red Topknot

Chinese Shoe of Violet Silk with Embroidery

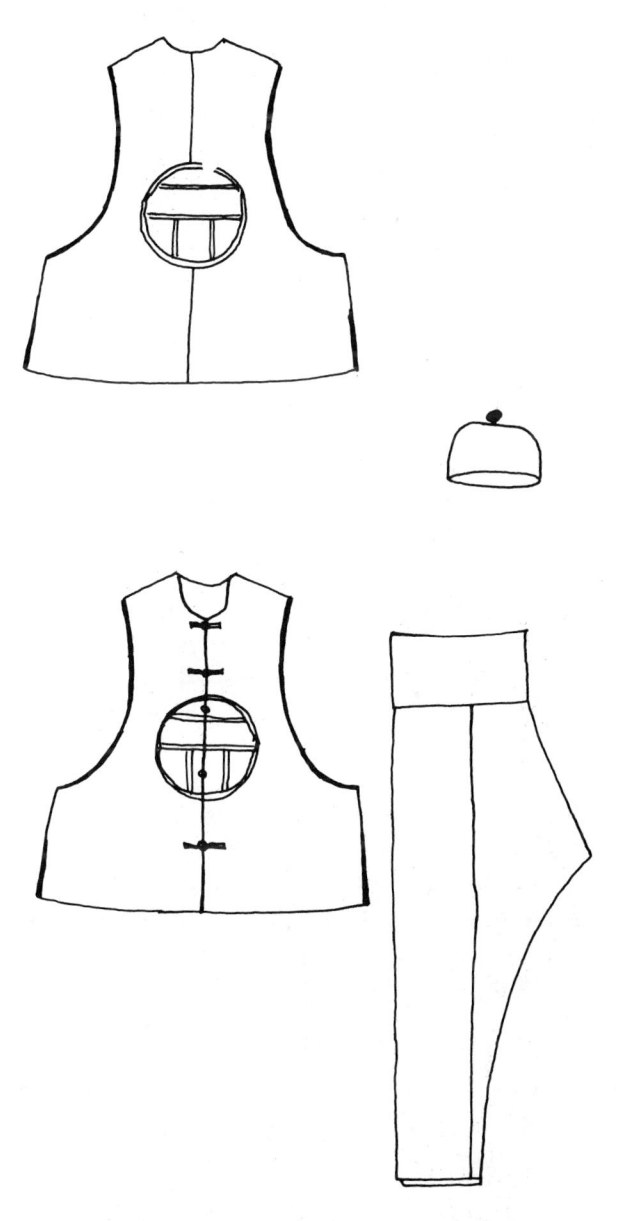

Chinese Man's Sleeveless Silk Jacket, Trousers, and Black Satin Cap

including dragons, which represented the emperor, the Son of Heaven.[6] The dragon robe styles survive today in theatrical costumes.

Korea

Western dress is worn in the urban areas of Korea. Traditional costume requires young married men and women to wear white—the men in trousers or pantaloons, a shirt and a sash, the women in a long, high-waisted skirt, a blouse, and a colored bolero with ribbons. See Figure 4-17. Wedding clothing is quite festive. The bride wears a brightly colored embroidered gown and a beaded crown. The groom layers a red topcoat over a white shirt and trousers. Older Korean males traditionally wear a long white coat that wraps and ties with ribbons on the right side, and also a brimmed, black horsehair hat.

Japan

In Japan Western clothing has been adopted by men and by more and more women, but the traditional costume can still be seen. The *kimono* is a full-sleeved robe that can be worn wrapped to the left and sashed by the *obi*, which is knotted in the back. It can also be worn open as an overcoat. A kimono can be made from plain cotton fabric, from print, from brocade or embroidered silk, or it can be quilted. See Figure 4-18. Kimonos can be layered. The women's outer kimono is shorter than the inner kimono. The man's outer kimono is also short and open like a coat. White-toed socks called *tabi* are worn with either *zori* (sandals), or *geta* (cork or wooden clogs). Elaborate headresses are worn today by the geishas. Highly elaborate costumes in the full Japanese tradition are still seen at the No Theatre.

---

[6] Walter A. Fairservis, Jr., *Costumes of the East* (New York: Am. Mus. Nat'l. History, 1971) p. 118.

Figure 4-17. Korean Costumes.

Korean Woven Straw Hat with Red Trim

Korean Jacket of Navy Blue with Multicolored Stripes and Trim

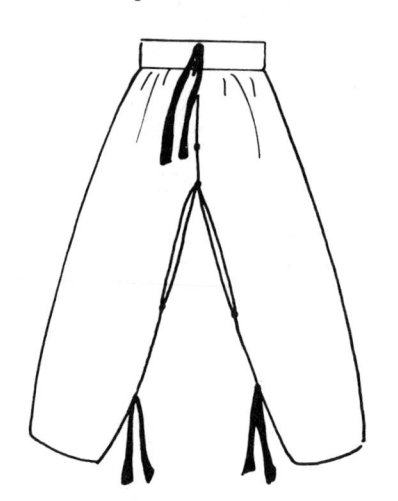

Korean Trousers of Red Cotton

Africa

The costumes of northern Africa—Morocco, Algeria, Tunisia, Libya—are very similar to those of the Middle East. The haik and chal-

National Costumes

war are worn by women of Algeria, and the caftan by women of Morocco. Men of the region wear the tobe, kibr, kamis, gandoura, aba, kaffiyeh (described under Middle East), and the fez and tarboosh. Another cloak in addition to the aba is the circular burnoose, which may be made with or without an attached hood. See Figure 4-19.

Traditional costumes of Ethiopia include a gandoura, a *chamma,* which is a togalike outer garment worn by men and women, and a one-piece, long-sleeve undergarment. In Senegal a stripped kibr goes over a tobe, and a multicolored skullcap can be worn.

The Bambara women of Mali wear a side wrapped striped skirt, a striped or printed

Figure 4-18. Japenese Silk Kimono with White Ground and Red/Blue/Green Flower Print.

94 Fashion: Color, Line, and Design

Figure 4-19. African Costumes.

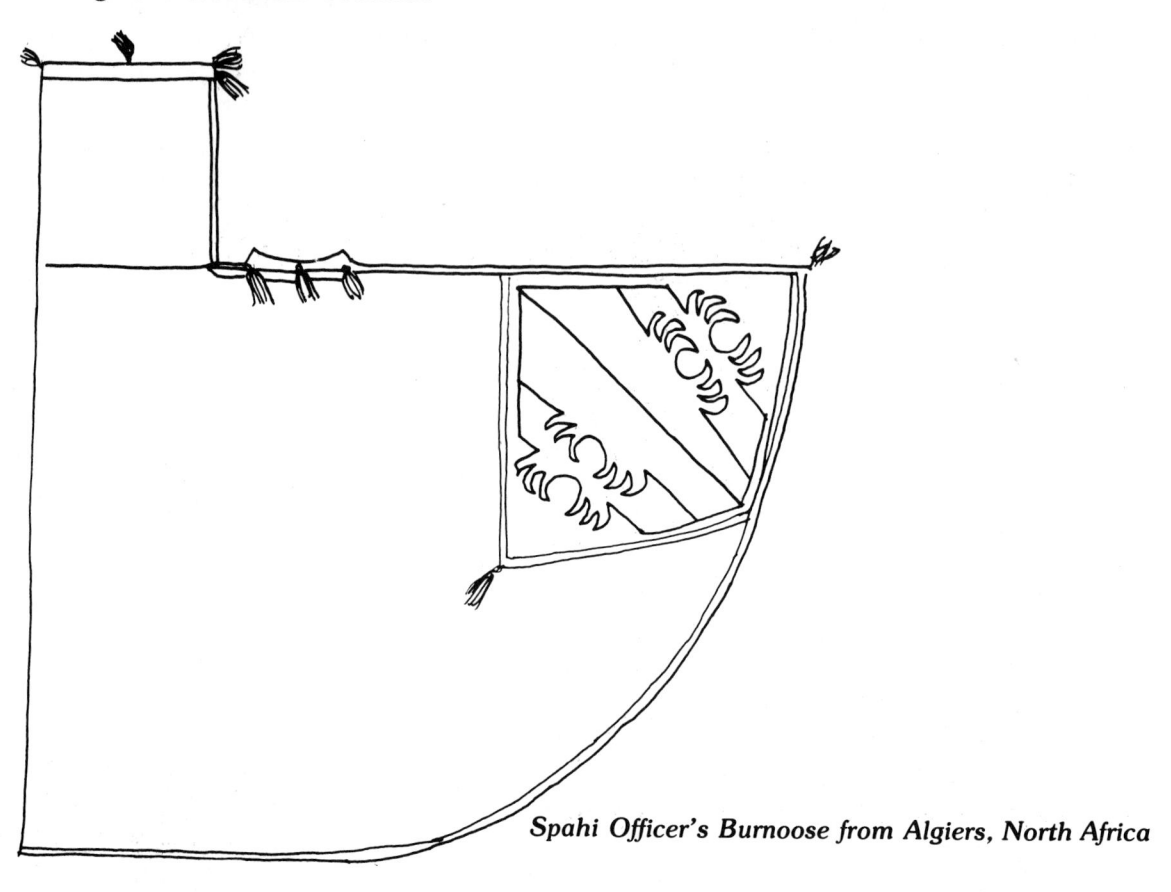

Spahi Officer's Burnoose from Algiers, North Africa

Gasabia and Hooded Jacket from Tunis, North Africa

National Costumes

sleeveless bodice, and a head scarf or turban. In Timbuktu, Mali, women wear a bold, bright, printed loose robe, the *boubou,* and a turban. Mali men wear an aba or a tobe with a turban or a *fez.*

Liberian women have multicolored printed skirts that are sometimes wrapped, print or solid blouses, and a turban. In Ghana, women also wear brightly printed fabric made into draped garments. In Ghana and in many other regions women wear their hair plaited or molded. Nigerian men wear the aba in camel hair, wool, or cotton over trousers and with a tarboosh.

Moslems in Kenya wear the tobe, the aba, and a white turban. The Masai women there have goatskin gowns, copper and iron wire jewelry, and shaved heads. In South Africa the Durban Indian's costume consists of a long white shirt called a *kurta* and a turban, the *pagri* (also worn in India). Zulu women wear a printed draped garment over a bodice. The traditional Zulu men's costume includes a cloak and a leopard headdress. Swazi women of Swaziland wear a draped black, white, and red geometric printed cloth knotted on one shoulder over a black skirt. The Swazi men wrap the patterned cloth around their waists.

United States of America

The United States was populated by emigrants from all over the world. Many brought their native dress, which can be seen at certain holidays or festivals. Others, like the Old Believers' Russian Community in Oregon, still wear the costumes of their heritage. Contemporary clothing predominates all over the country, and therefore the only native costumes that will be covered here are those of the American Indian, the Eskimo, and the Hawaiian.

There is one item of apparel that can be classified as indigenous to the United States, and that is the denim jean. The first pair of jeans was made by Levi Strauss in 1850. They were made from heavy denim to meet the clothing needs of California gold miners. Today jeans are made in many fabrics, colors, and styles and are worn by men, women, and children all over the world.

The American Indians are the original inhabitants of the United States, but the number of tribes has decreased and the size of tribes has diminished as a result of wars, disease, and conflicts with government processes. Although many Indians have assimilated into Anglo-American culture, others restrict their lives to reservations. American dress has been adopted on reservations except for certain articles of tribal dress that are still worn regularly. Traditional tribal costume survives, surfacing for special events.

The Indian costumes are almost always made of tanned hides. The most common articles of costume include a shirt or tunic, leggings, moccasins, and a headdress. The men's costume often includes a breechcloth and the women's some type of skirt. Fringe is important on hems, seams, sleeves, and leggings. Beadwork, quills, or shells decorate the tunic, belts, and moccasins. Fur, hair, and feathers might also be used on the garments. Woven blankets, tanned hides, or fur skins serve as robes in the winter in cold climates. Headdress ranges from simple headbands to elaborate feathered war bonnets, and beaded, silver, or turquoise jewelry is used for adornment.

The costumes of each tribe vary according to climate and other location influences. Hair style, beadwork, or headdress are all used to distinguish one tribe from another. The Seminoles of Florida wear cotton—the women wearing a multicolored flounced skirt and top, and the men a shirt and trousers. Navajo Indians of New Mexico, Arizona, and Utah wear belted, bright velveteen smocks over skirts for women or pants for men. Zuni and Hopi women of New Mexico and Arizona wear black homespun dresses.

The native population of Alaska includes the Eskimos, Aleuts, and Indians. The traditional dress of these people incorporates a hooded parka, a shirt, breeches, and boots, all made of fur and skins for warmth. Sealskin was the most common, but bear, wolf, and fox skins were also used. Today mass-produced garments have replaced many of the homemade ones.

The best known Hawaiian native costume is the green ti-leaf skirt, printed wrapped bodice, and flowered leis, worn by the hula dancers. The floral printed full shift or *muu muu* is seen on the streets along with current American fashions.

Mexico

Before the Spaniard Cortez invaded Mexico in 1519, there was an extensive and highly developed Indian culture. The Spanish and other European invaders destroyed much of the early culture, but European influences did eventually blend with the Indian culture. The native dress is basically Indian, although some articles of Spanish costumes, such as the manton, were adapted by the upper class. Today modern dress is seen on the streets in the cities, but the traditional costumes can be seen in the small towns and at festivals.

Many articles of the Indian dress are cut in geometric shapes, for example, skirts are often rectangular (with front pleats and a belt) and stoles triangular. See Figure 4-20. Black is a popular background color, as it displays well the bright colors that are widely used. White is common in the peasant or peon dress. See Figure 4-21. The following are important items of Mexican traditional costume.

Serape—a man's straight shawl that is usually fringed, and often striped.

Poncho—a man's rectangular blanket-like coat with open sides that is put on over the head. It can be striped and fringed. See Figure 4-20.

Rebozo—a woman's shawl, often fringed.

Quechquemetl—a triangular, stitched stole that can be embroidered. See Figure 4-20.

Huipil Grande—a Tehuantepec woman's stiff, pleated white cotton and lace holiday headdress that is worn closed like a cape or open and hanging down the back. It is said to be adapted from the clothes of a baby rescued from the sea.

Alpargatas—peasant sandals, usually of canvas with hemp soles.

Sombrero—a wide-brimmed hat, usually of straw for the peasant. The gentleman often wears a felt sombrero.

China Poblana—the costume worn by the female dancer of *jarabe tapatio*, Mexico's national dance. The costume includes an embroidered white blouse and an embroidered and spangled red and green skirt. The embroidery comes from the legendary Chinese Princess (China Poblana) who was rescued from pirates by a Mexican ship.[7]

Charro—the costume worn by the male dancer of *jarabe tapatio*, consisting of tight black trousers and a short jacket embroidered in gold or silver, a bright serape, and a felt sombrero with gold or silver braid.

Central and South America

The countries of Central and South America had many different Indian cultures ranging

---

[7]Dorothy Gladys Spicer and Jolanda Bartas, *Latin American Costumes* (New York: Hyperion Press, 1941), p. 58.

National Costumes

from primitive ones to the highly developed one of the Incas. As in Mexico, European colonization developed these countries but destroyed much of their Indian culture. The colonialists influenced the native dress, especially the Spanish. Western style clothing is worn throughout Central and South America today, but native costume is still seen in the back country and, as in Mexico, for festivals. *Gauchos* are the cowboys of Argentina and Uruguay, whose traditional dress includes the chiripá (described below), loose pantaloons, boots, a short jacket, a brimmed felt hat, and spurs. A *chola* is a mixed-blood Bolivian

Figure 4-20. Mexican and Central and South American Costumes.

Yalalog Ceremonial Coat from Mexico

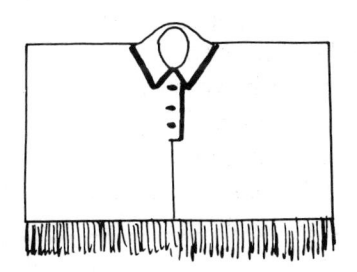

Thick Cranberry Wool Poncho from Ecuador

Embroidered Poncho from Guatemala

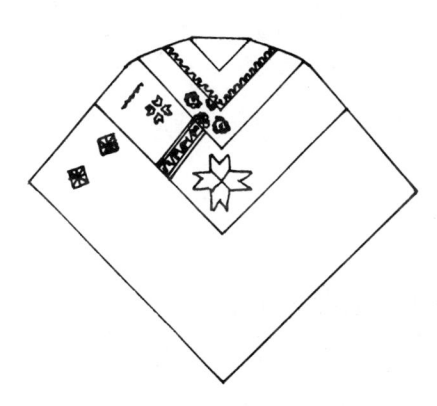

Mexican Huochil

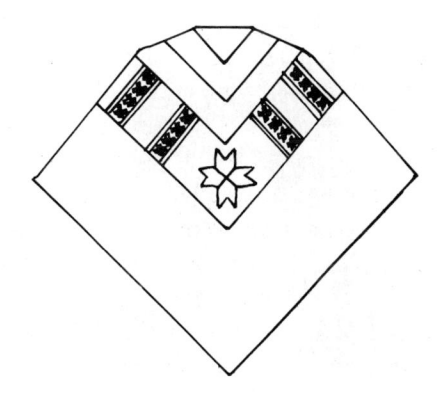

Indian Quechquemetl

woman who wears layers of bright skirts, a bright shawl, high-heeled boots, and a felt or straw derby.

The Panama hat is a commonly known item of Central and South American costume. It is made of palm fiber in Ecuador and Colombia but is sold and worn in Panama. In Ecuador a hard, molded, white felt hat with a brim is worn by men and women. Aymará Indians of Bolivia wear knitted skullcaps with

Figure 4-21. Mexican Costumes.

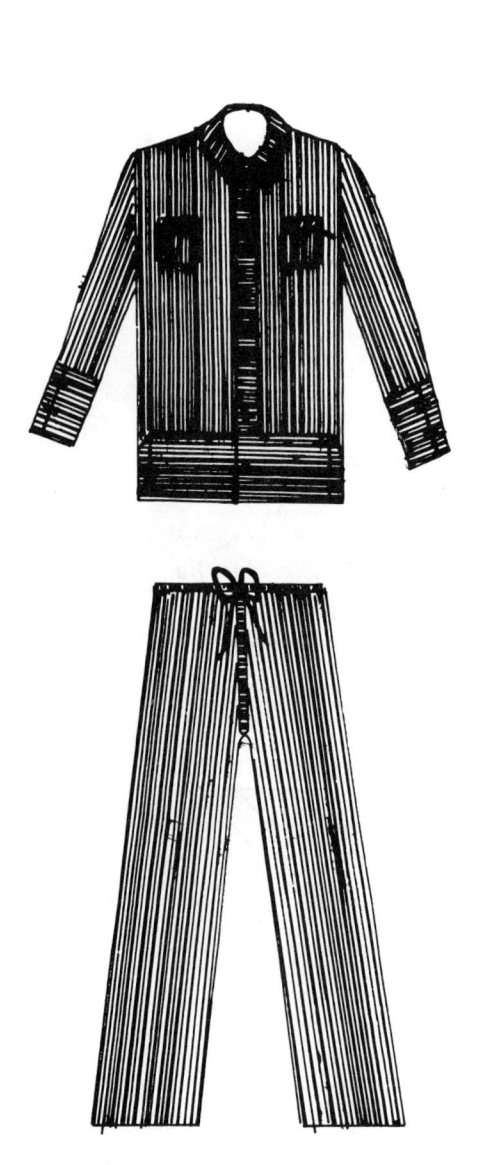

Mexican Stiffened Lace Blouse with Red Satin Trim

Mexican Man's Cotton Ticking Shirt and Trousers in Pink/Black/White

Mexican Shirred and Embroidered Camisa

National Costumes

earflaps; another wool cap with earflaps comes from the Cuzco region of Peru.

Homespun wool, usually of llama or guanaco wool, is a common fabric. Cotton is used in the warmer climates, especially for shirts. Black and white are important background colors. Bright colors often appear as striping or embroidery. See Figure 4-22.

Some important Central and South American costume items are:

Poncho — (see Mexico). Ponchos are worn throughout Latin America, in short or quite long lengths. They are usually made of wool and can be plain, embroidered, striped, or fringed.

Rebozo — (see Mexico). Rebozos are

Figure 4-22. Central and South American Costumes.

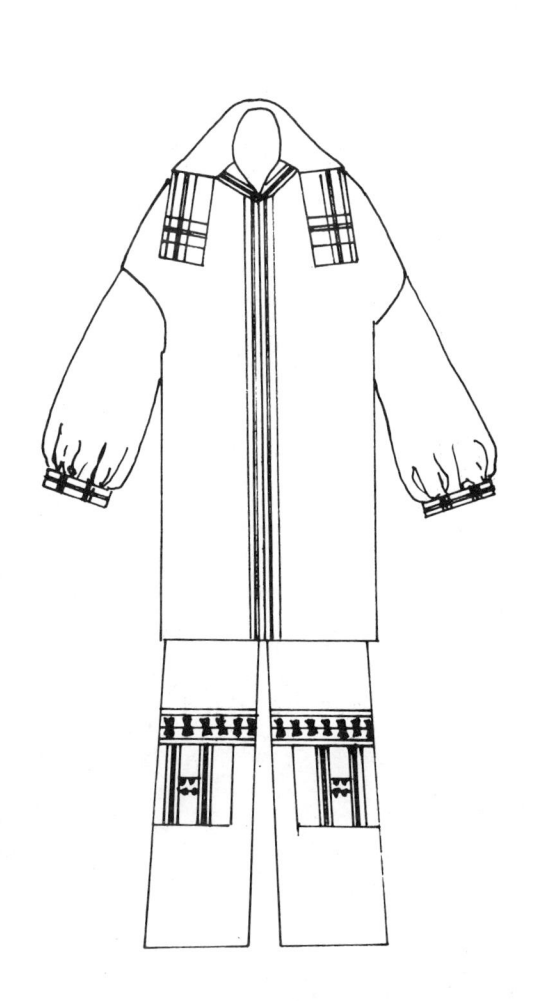

Guatemalan Embroidered Shirt and Trousers

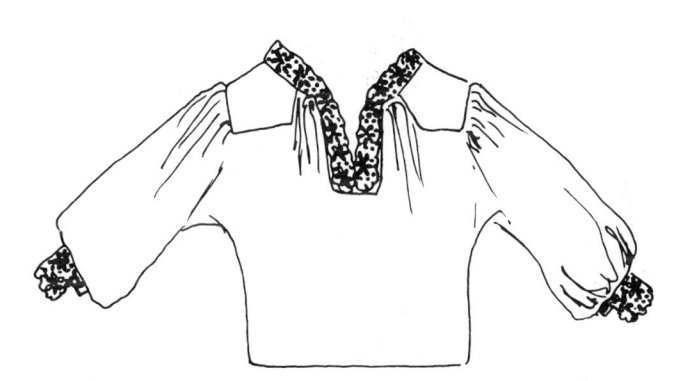

Bolivian Blouse of White Cotton with Eyelet

Bolivian Yellow Cotton Twill Skirt with Shirring

worn by women in Guatemala, Ecuador, and Bolivia, often to hold their babies or bundles.

Serape — (see Mexico). Serapes are worn by men in Ecuador, Bolivia, and Peru.

Pollera — an elaborate, long, off-the-shoulder dress with ruffles, flounces, lace trim, and embroidery from Panama.

Huipil — a woman's blouse from Guatemala that is often embroidered and worn layered.

Tzute — a turbanlike headdress worn by men and women in Guatemala. It can also serve as a shawl or baby carrier.

Chiripá — a skirtlike garment wrapped around the hips and held by a belt. It is worn by the cowboys or gauchos of Argentina and Uruguay and the huasos of Chile.

Projects for National Costumes

1. Research a particular culture and write a report on the costumes of the culture. Include footnotes, a bibliography, illustrations.
2. Study current fashions. Using illustrations from newspapers and magazines identify styles that might have been influenced by national costumes.
3. Visit large and small local retailers. Find out if any of them are selling native costumes as regular clothing. If so, are the clothes in a separate location with special identification? Are there any stores that limit their stock to national dress?

Bibliography

Bradshaw, Angela. **World Costumes.** Great Britain: The Macmillan Co., 1961.

Fairservis, Walter A., Jr. **Costumes of the East.** New York: Am. Mus. Nat'l. History, 1971.

Gerster, George. "River of Sorrow, River of Hope." **National Geographic** 145 #2: 152-189.

Mann, Kathleen. **Peasant Costume in Europe.** London: Adam and Charles Block, 1950.

Onassis, Jacqueline, ed. **In the Russian Style.** New York: The Viking Press, 1977.

Roach, Mary Ellen, and Eicher, Joanne Bubolz, eds. **Dress, Adornment, and the Social Order.** New York: John Wiley & Sons, Inc., 1965.

Seton, Julia M. **The Indian Costume Book.** Santa Fe, New Mexico: The Seton Village Press, 1938.

Spicer, Dorothy Gladys, and Bartas, Jolanda. **Latin American Costumes.** New York: The Hyperion Press, 1941.

Wentzel, Volkmar. "Zulu King Weds a Swazi Princess." **National Geographic** 153 #1: 46-61.

Wilcox, R. Turner. **Folk and Festival Costume of the World.** New York: Charles Scribner's Sons, 1965.

Wilcox, R. Turner. **The Dictionary of Costume.** New York: Charles Scribner's Sons, 1963.

5

Design Motifs

Clothing and accessories are often decorated with design motifs. Some motifs are cut out, as in eyelet, lace, a scalloped hem, or a garment with a hole cut out to create a pattern; others are printed onto the fabric, or are woven or knitted into the fabric. Motifs come from geometric, natural, and free or abstract forms. Many motifs used today come from the classical periods of Egypt, Greece, and Rome. Two or more motifs can be combined to form intricate patterns. The patterns are successful if they *contribute* to the total design of the clothing or accessory rather than *dominate* it.

Straight and Curved Lines

The simplest design form is the line. Lines can be perfectly straight (as drawn with a ruler), curved, broken, or bent to form angles. They can be thick or thin. Lines can be placed vertically, horizontally, or diagonally. Lines can be combined into new motifs such as arrows or zigzags. See Figure 5-1 or 5-4. Lines can be used in designs to create illusions.

Just as color is subjectively perceived, so are lines. Vertical lines connote strength. They slim and add height. Horizontal lines connote calmness, perhaps because they appear to be lying down, or because a still water surface or a flat land surface has a horizontal line. Horizontal lines add width. Diagonal lines connote action, leading the eye. Curved lines and spirals create movement. Concave (interior curve of a sphere) lines seem to contract and appear hard with distinct edges. Convex (exterior curve of a sphere) lines seem to expand and appear soft with indefinite edges. Forms made with convex lines tend to be more popular. Thick lines are bold while thin ones are delicate. The S-shaped curve, or *ogee,* is called the line of beauty. Apparel designed with S curves is flattering to the wearer and appealing to the eye. The reverse of the S curve is called the *cyma* (SI-ma). See Figure 5-2.

When the ends of a line come together to enclose an area, a shape is formed. Shapes used in design motifs are two dimensional and can be outlined, solid, transparent, colored, or textured. Shapes are geometric, representational (florals or animals), and nonrepresentational (freeform).

Geometric Shapes

Geometric shapes are the basis for many design motifs. The most common are squares, rectangles, triangles, and circles. Variations of these forms are cylinders, cones, diamonds, and ovals. Polygons (forms with more than four sides and four angles) are also seen as design motifs; the pentagon (five sides), the hexagon (six sides), and the octagon (eight sides) are examples. Five- and six-pointed stars are derivations of the pentagon and hexagon. See Figure 5-3. Discussion of how to repeat a selected shape to create a fabric design can be found in Chapter 6.

Rectangular forms are used in three of the major classical border motifs. The simplest is the *dentil,* which is a row of upright rectan-

Figure 5-1. Lines Are the Simplest Form of Design.

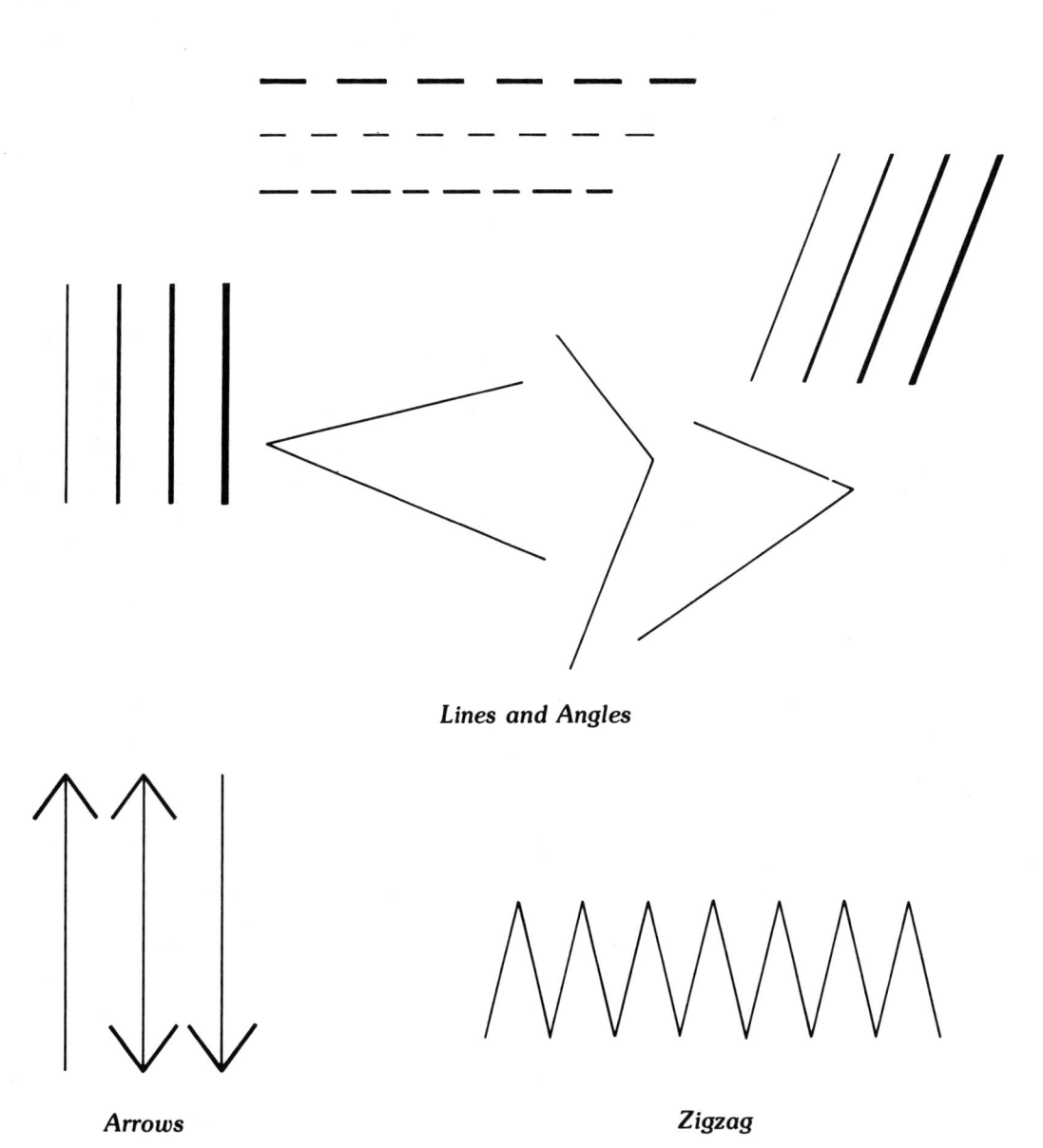

Lines and Angles

Arrows

Zigzag

Design Motifs 105

gles. Dentil comes from the French word "dent," meaning "tooth." The *fret,* or *Greek key,* is based on rectangles, with their horizontal and vertical lines extending to form new right angles. The *embattled border* is also derived from rectangles (or squares) and is similar to the stonework pattern found on castle turrets. See Figure 5-4. In clothing this pattern is referred to as "castellated edges" (see Middle Ages section of Chapter 3).

Triangular forms can be seen in the *chevron,* a series of triangles in a zigzag pattern. See Figure 5-5. The cone shape often used in fabric designs is derived from the triangle.

Circular motifs include the circle, semicircle, sphere, oval, and cylinder. Also included are *domes* (variations on the sphere), *medallions* (circular or oval motifs), and *rosettes* (circular motifs with a floral pattern). *Beading* is a border of circles or semicircles. It can also be an eyelet embroidery or lace trim with circular holes through which ribbon is drawn. The *scallop* border is a line of connecting semicircles. Scallops are also seen on the edges of the *shell,* a fanlike motif. The *meander* is a border of semicircles alternating up and down. *Scroll* motifs are circular spirals. They are seen in the *wave*

Figure 5-2. Lines Are Subjectively Perceived.

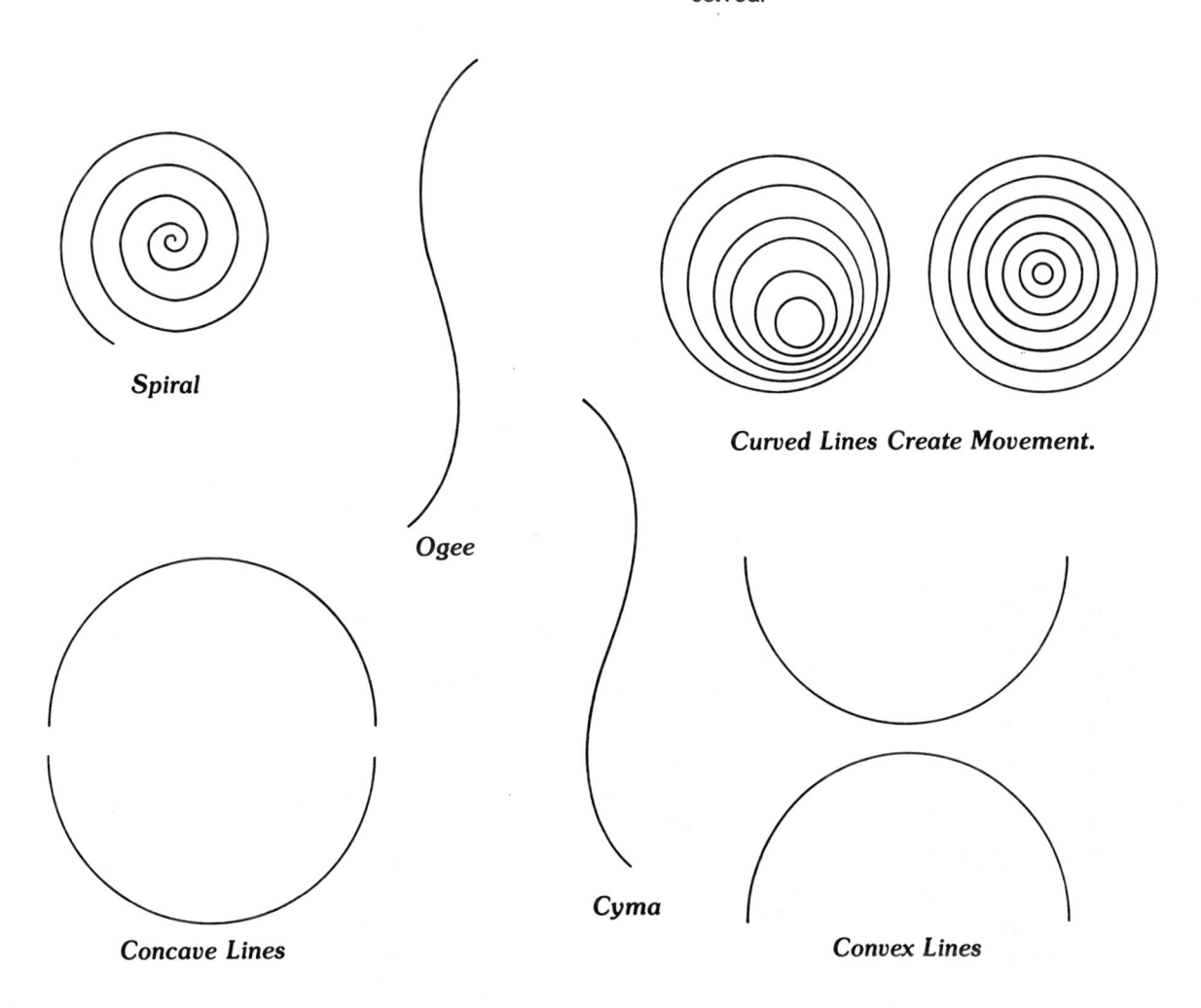

Spiral

Ogee

Curved Lines Create Movement.

Concave Lines

Cyma

Convex Lines

border, which combines an S curve placed horizontally with a scroll at each end of the curve. The *running scroll* has the scroll only on one end of the horizontal S curve. The pattern alternates one curve and scroll pointing up with one pointing down. The *chain* motif has interlocking circles or ovals. The *rope* or *cable* motif consists of overlapping S curves.

Figure 5-3. Geometric Shapes Are the Basis for Many Design Motifs.

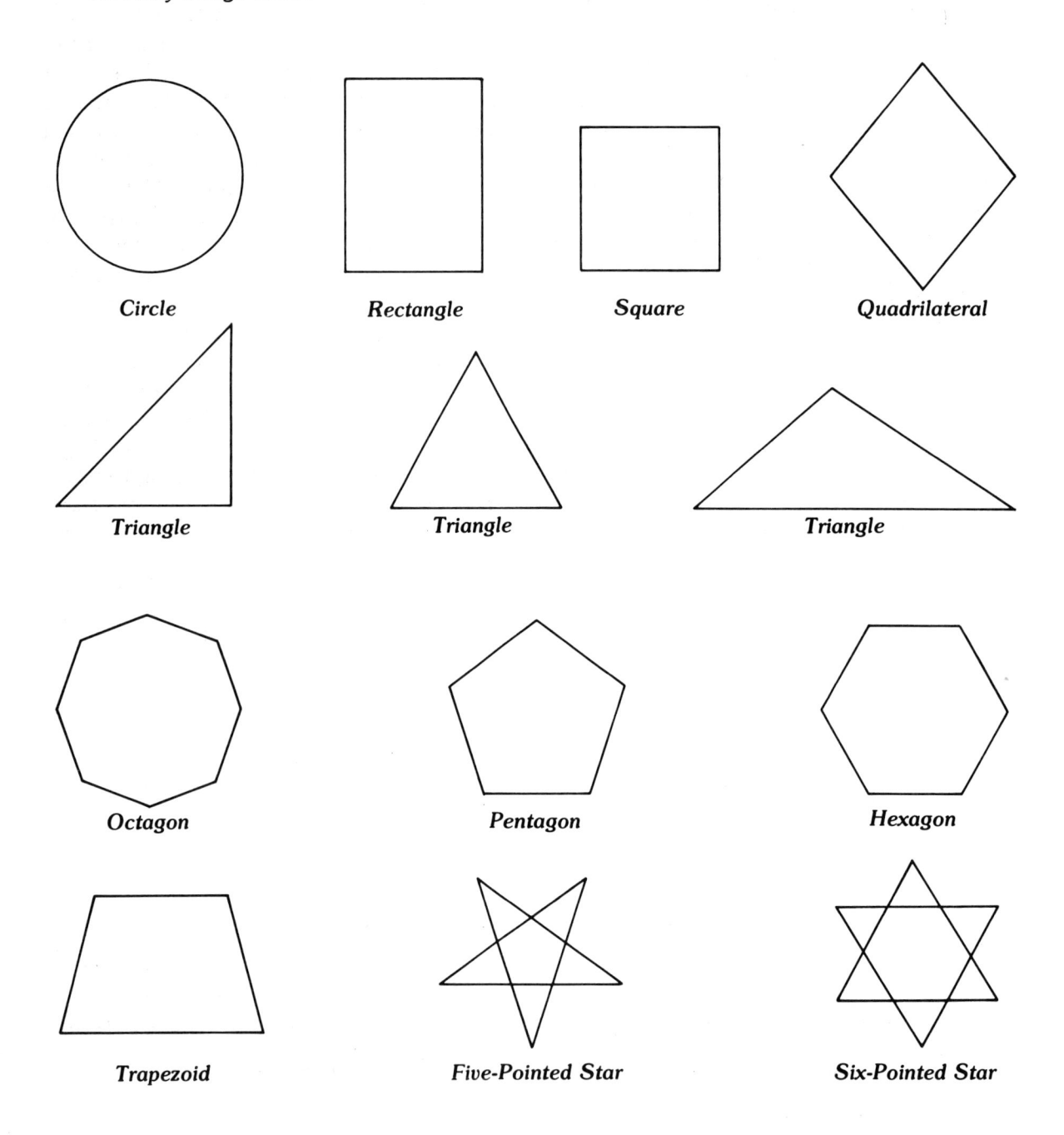

Circle *Rectangle* *Square* *Quadrilateral*

Triangle *Triangle* *Triangle*

Octagon *Pentagon* *Hexagon*

Trapezoid *Five-Pointed Star* *Six-Pointed Star*

Design Motifs

The *egg and dart motif* alternates ovals with triangular arrow points. See Figure 5-6 for illustrations of the motifs.

Shapes from Nature

Many design motifs come from nature, in organic forms of flowers, leaves, trees, vegetables, fruits, animals, and people, and in inorganic or nonliving forms of snowflakes, rocks, mountains, water, and clouds. The designer can use the object exactly the way it appears in nature or stylize the object by simplifying the form, creating a fanciful version, elaborating the form, or innovating with coloration. The motif can also be an abstract interpretation.

The use of flowers and leaves as design motifs goes back to ancient times. The *lotus* pattern, from Egypt, resembles palm leaves. The *Greek lily* is an elongated lily shape. The *anthemion* is a heart-shaped motif containing leaves, and is often combined with the Greek lily. The *acanthus* is a large, curled leaf first used in Corinthian architecture by the Greeks.

Other motifs came from later periods, for example the *fleur-de-lis,* which is the French version of the lily. It was used in the coat-of-arms of Charles V. The *quatrefoil* is a four-leaf motif, and the *tetrafoil* is a three-leaf motif used in medieval Gothic decoration. See Figure 5-7 for illustrations of these motifs.

Flowers in designs can be presented individually, in clusters or in a variety of ways, including these: a *bouquet,* or bunch of flowers; a *garland*, or floral wreath; a *festoon,* or looped garlands. Some popular flowers used in design motifs are daisies, roses, lilies, and tulips. One design will have a readily identifiable flower whereas another will have an entirely inventive one. A flower shown from the front will look different than the same flower shown from the center out to the petals. Certain flowers lend themselves to geometric interpretations better than others, for example daisies, created with circles.

Leaves, stems, or vines can contribute to a floral motif or create designs by themselves. Borders are often created from simple or elaborate combinations of vines and leaves. Trees, fruits, and vegetables provide many other sources for design motifs. Some motifs

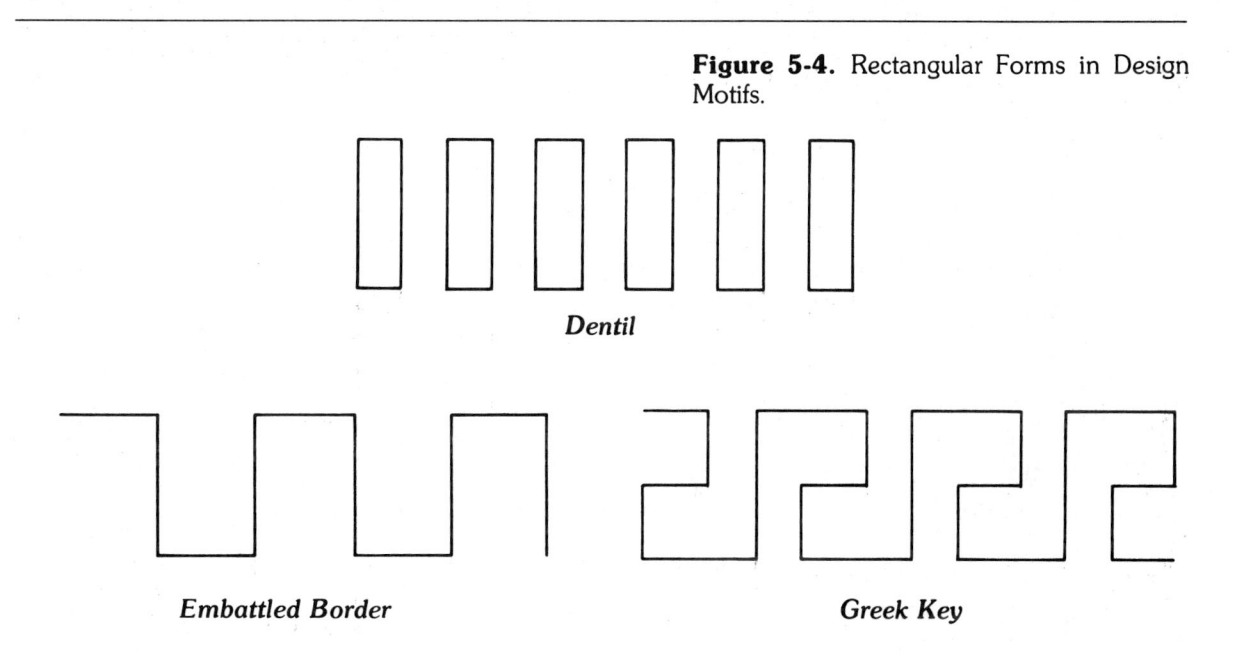

Figure 5-4. Rectangular Forms in Design Motifs.

Dentil

Embattled Border

Greek Key

Figure 5-5. Triangular Form in Design Motifs.

Chevron or Zigzag

have become associated with specific themes, as in cactus motifs for Western designs and pineapples and palm trees for Hawaiian designs. See Figure 5-8 for use of trees, birds, animals, people and houses in a design motif.

Animal, fish, and bird motifs go back to ancient times. Generally a culture will choose an animal indigenous to the locale for use in the design motifs. Animals often had a religious connotation for primitive and ancient people. The animal forms in the Zodiac — Pisces the fish, Aries the ram, Taurus the bull, Cancer the crab, Leo the Lion, Scorpio the scorpion, Sagittarius the centaur, and Capricorn the goat — have been used over and over as design motifs. The lion is popular and has been shown in many forms, as has the ram. Popular birds include eagles, peacocks, ducks, swans, and roosters. The dolphin, crab, conch, and scallop shell are often used, as are fish and shellfish.

Mythical animals have also been used as design motifs. Included in this group are the Egyptian sphinx (body of a lion; head of a hawk, ram, or man), the Greek centaur (head, arms, and body of a man; trunk and legs of a horse), the griffin (head and wings of an eagle; body and legs of a lion), and the unicorn (a horselike animal with one horn growing from the forehead).

The human form, either realistic or stylized has been an important source for design motifs. Some human motifs use historic figures. Others use cartoon figures. The motifs can show the entire body or they can show parts of the body, such as heads or hands. The human body can be used alone or in combination with flora, fauna, or other objects.

Freeform or Nonrepresentational Shapes

Freeform shapes can have a base in geometrics, for example, a pattern made up of spotty or blotchy shapes could be considered derivative of circles. Freeform shapes might be linear — derivative of straight, curved, broken, thick, thin, or irregular lines. Or they might be shapes created by the designer that are totally unique and free. If a motif is based on a form from nature, it is considered to be representational, even if the motif is rendered in such an abstract manner that it is hard to identify the subject. Geometric forms are nonrepresentational.

Combinations of Motifs

Different motifs can be combined to create new ones. Some of the more common combinations include florals in stripes and animals in medallions. Basic geometric forms can be put together for complex motifs. All of the animal forms can be combined with all of the plant forms. The variety of design motifs is endless.

Design Motifs 109

Figure 5-6. Circular Forms in Design Motifs.

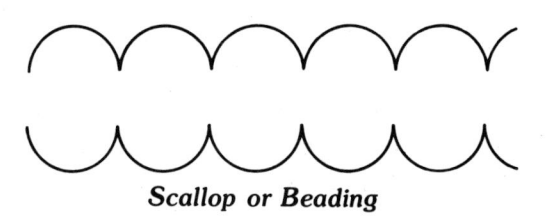

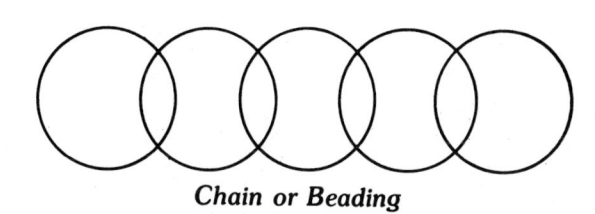

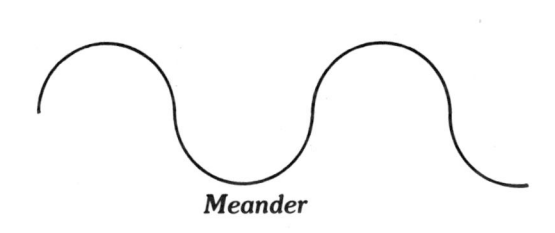

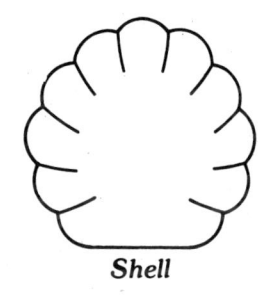

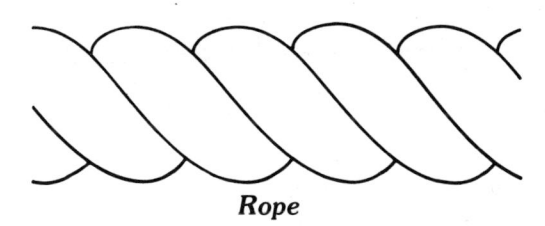

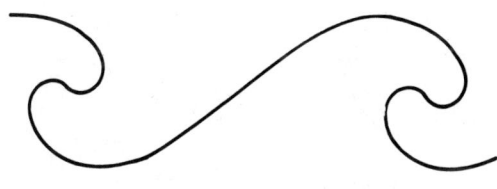

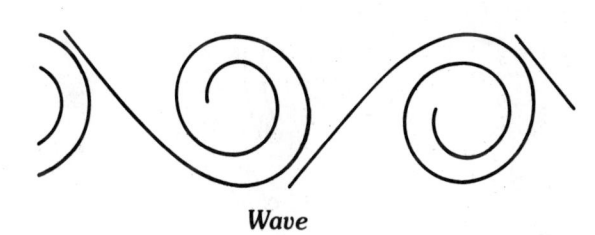

Scallop or Beading

Chain or Beading

Meander

Shell

Rosette

Rope

Egg and Dart

Running Scroll

Wave

Figure 5-7. The Use of Flowers and Leaves as Design Motifs Dates Back to Ancient Times.

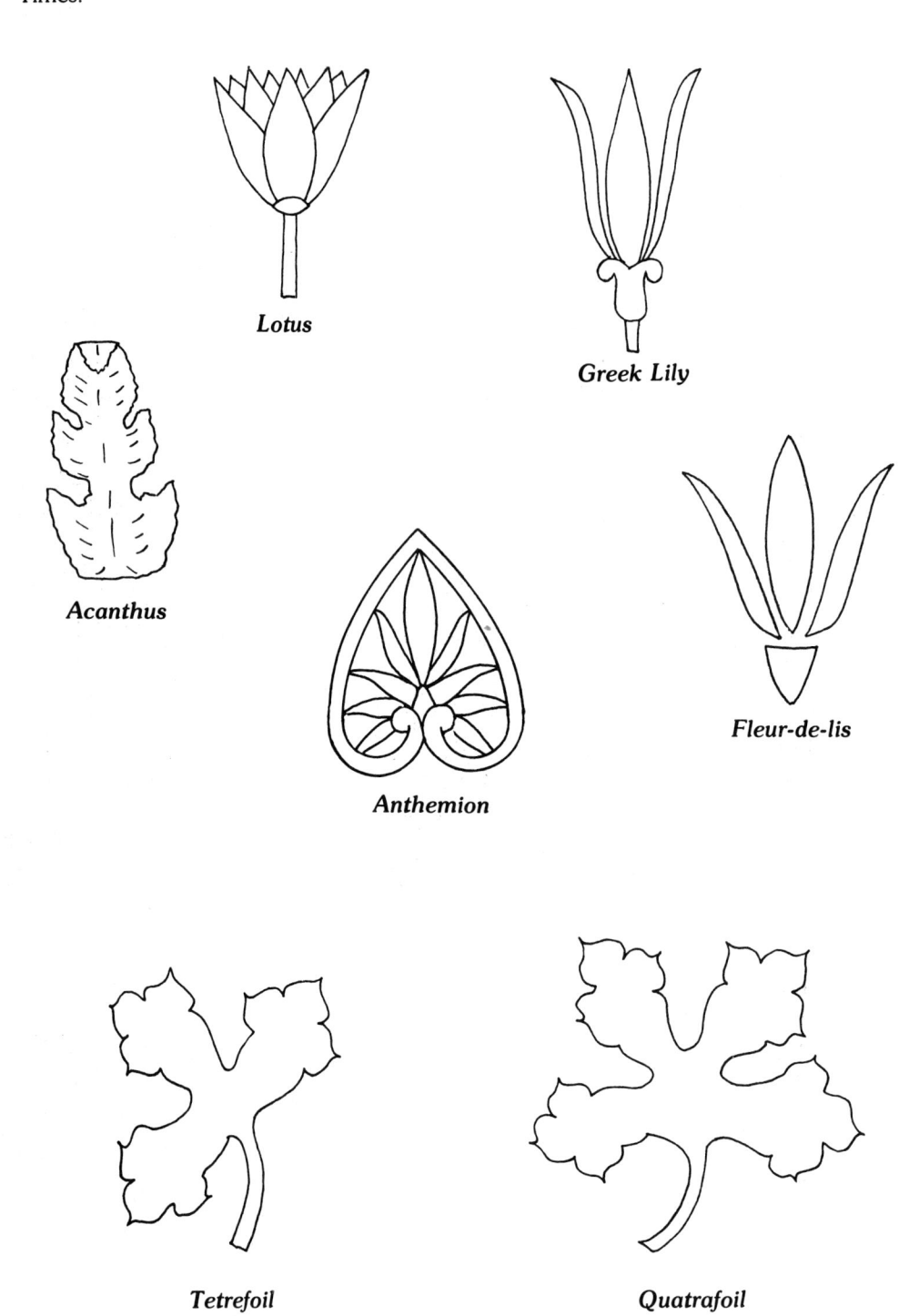

Lotus

Greek Lily

Acanthus

Anthemion

Fleur-de-lis

Tetrefoil

Quatrafoil

Design Motifs 111

Figure 5-8. "Columbia Primitive" Design by Fieldcrest Combines Trees, Birds, Animals, People, and Houses.

Projects for Design Motifs

1. Choose one of the following areas and research the history of the motif. Include illustrations.
   A. Animal, bird, or fish motifs
   B. Floral motifs
   C. Mythological beast motifs
   D. Oriental motifs
   E. Heraldry motifs
   F. Art Deco motifs

2. Create a design motif for six of the following categories:
   A. Lines
   B. Circles
   C. Squares
   D. Rectangles
   E. Triangles
   F. Floral
   G. Animals, birds, or fish
   H. Human
   I. Combination of forms

Bibliography

Alexander, Mary Jean. **Handbook of Decorative Design and Ornament.** New York: L. Amièl Publishing Co., 1965.

Anderson, Donald M. **Elements of Design.** New York: Holt, Rinehart & Winston, 1961.

Bates, Kenneth F. **Basic Design: Principles and Practice.** New York: Funk & Wagnalls, 1975.

Best-Mangard, Adolfo. **A Method for Creative Design.** New York: Knopf, Inc. 1926.

Ernst, James A. **Drawing the Line.** New York: Reinhold Publishing Corp., 1962.

Malcolm, Dorothea C. **Design: Elements and Principles.** Worcester, Mass.: Davis Publications, Inc., 1972.

Metzig, William. **Heraldry for the Designer.** New York: Van Nostrand Reinhold Co., 1970.

Wolchonok, Louis. **Design for Artists and Craftsmen.** New York: Dover Publications, Inc., 1953.

6 Fabric Design

A Successful Design

A successful fabric design is harmonious and pleasing to the eye and suits the item of apparel or home furnishings without overwhelming it. There should be a rhythmic flow to the design that is maintained after the fabric is used to construct a garment or home furnishings item. A good designer will try to make sure the design is not distorted by the way the fabric is used. Fabric used for apparel can be cut, stitched, pieced, draped, pleated, tucked, or gathered. Fabric used for home furnishings can be used flat, draped, quilted, tucked, or tufted. Figure 6-1 illustrates how a simple repeat of lines lends itself well to the large scale and to the quilting and draping used for bedroom furnishings.

The fabric designer usually does not know the exact application the fabric will have. Some fabric designers limit their work to specific markets such as home furnishings. Other designers create in a studio that sells the designs to many different types of fabric companies. There are couture designers who develop their own fabrics directly with a mill or work very closely with fabric designers. Often a fabric design will be for exclusive use by an apparel manufacturer, designer, or home furnishings manufacturer.

Balance is an important element in design. The design can be *symmetrical* (evenly distributed) or *asymmetrical* (unevenly distributed). The design can also be *radial* (moving out from a central point) as shown in Figure 6-2.

The design motifs can take the form of a *border* or an *allover* pattern. A border pattern is shown in Figure 6-3. Note also the design bordering the wooden chest and the design on the two porcelain jars. An allover pattern is the result of repeating the design motif over the entire fabric, as shown in Figure 6-4.

Repeat of The Design

The design motif is the basic entity, but the success of the motif as a fabric design depends greatly on how it is repeated. There are many different ways to repeat a motif. The simplest method forms a block pattern with the motif repeating in parallel rows both vertically and horizontally. Another method drops the motif by half of its size, by a quarter of its size, or by other fractional amounts. Another method is to repeat in a diamond layout. By reversing the design motif, alternating repeats are created. The motif can be alternated horizontally, vertically, or both horizontally and

Figure 6-1. "Classic Chromatic Stripes" Design by Fieldcrest Is a Simple Repeat of Lines.

Fabric Design

vertically. The design motif can also be repeated on a diagonal line or turned in different directions horizontally and vertically before the entire pattern is repeated. See Figure 6-5 for illustrations of these repeat methods. These repeat methods can be used individually for a simple design, or they can be combined for a complex design. For example, the designer can alternate the motif vertically in a diamond layout (see Figure 6-6).

Some motifs cover a wide area and have a great amount of detail. Finding the repeat in such a design can be quite difficult (see Figure 6-7 showing the combination of geometric shapes, flowers, violins, and hearts). It is also necessary to decide how each repeat will join with the previous one. The repeats might join end to end; one might go into the space of the other without touching it; they might overlap. The design and repeat must be suitable for the width of the finished fabric. Most apparel fabrics are between 36 and 54 inches wide. Most home furnishings fabrics are between 45 and 60 inches wide. Fabrics originally designed for either the apparel or home furnishings market are sometimes suitable for the other market as well.

Colors of the Design

It is not enough to have a motif and a well-balanced repeat arrangement. A successful fabric design must also have an appealing color scheme. A fabric can be printed in just one coloration or in several colorations. The designer works up the fabric in the main coloration, and then small matched segments are done in the alternate colorations.

There are many principles and limitations to consider before coloring a fabric design. Much of what was discussed in Chapter 1 on color can be applied here. The color scheme and the design should be harmonious. The

Figure 6-2. A Radial Design Moves Out from a Central Point.

potential uses of the fabric should be considered. If the fabric will be used in seasonal apparel, the colors might be chosen accordingly. Fashion trends are not limited to just the clothing silhouette, but also include the fabric design and colors. The method of applying the design to the cloth might limit the number of colors that can be used. The texture of the cloth can affect the intensity of the colors, for example the shine of satin increases the intensity. Color on sheer fabric looks different from the same color on opaque fabric. If the print is on a dark background, the colors look different from the same colors on a white or light background. Outlining the design can also affect the color.

After the design motif, repeat method, and color scheme have been determined, a complete rendering in color is necessary. The coloring medium is very important. If the fabric will be printed with dyes, then drawing ink, colored soft-tip pens, or fabric dye can be used by the designer in the rendering. The latter media all produce transparent color, meaning one color can be printed on top of another to produce a third color.

In the printing process, each color might be applied in a different step. If this is the case, the designer breaks down the design for

Figure 6-3. "Classic Chromatic Lace" Design by Fieldcrest Is a Border Pattern.

Fabric Design

Figure 6-4. "Halston's Circle H" Design by Fieldcrest Is an Allover Pattern.

Figure 6-5. Repeat Methods in Fabric Design.

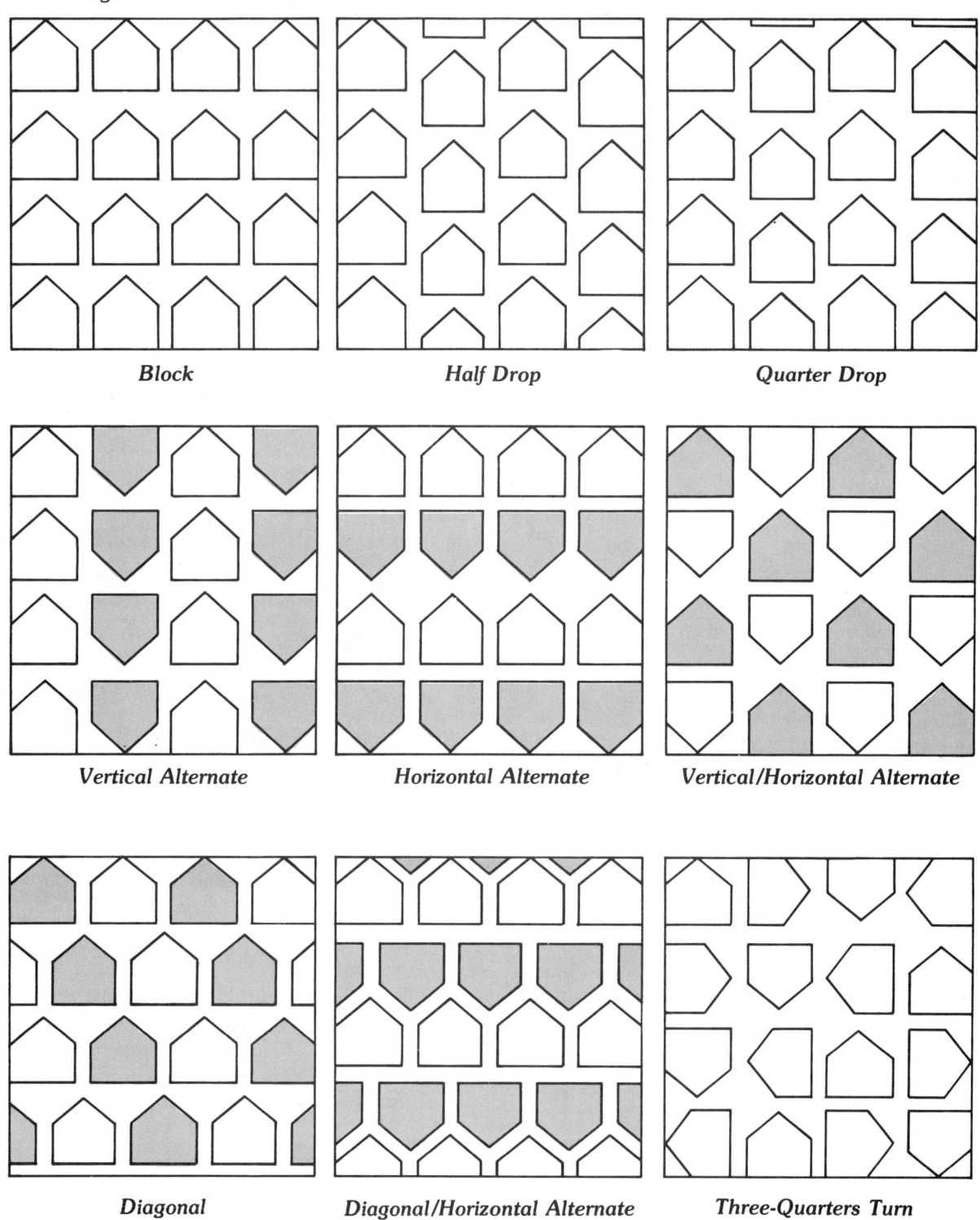

Block

Half Drop

Quarter Drop

Vertical Alternate

Horizontal Alternate

Vertical/Horizontal Alternate

Diagonal

Diagonal/Horizontal Alternate

Three-Quarters Turn

Fabric Design

each color creating *color separations*. Each color separation is done on tracing paper. Registration marks ensure that each part of the colored design is properly lined up, and thus the entire motif is easily repeated.

The design and the coloration in combination create a textured effect on the fabric. The designer must consider this textural result carefully, because the fabric might have a textured surface. The visual texture of the design and the texture of the cloth should be harmonious.

Fabric designers have usually studied art before beginning their careers. There are college and art school programs specifically for textile design. A good designer is a creative person who is attentive to detail, and has a thorough knowledge of textile history and a keen sense of color harmony.

History of Fabric Printing

Printing a design onto fabric has a long history. Printing stamps from Mesopotamia, sculpture from Babylonia and Assyria, and murals from Egypt indicate that cloth may have been printed 5000 years ago, although there are no such fabrics extant.[8] Printing blocks from India dated as early as 3000 B.C. have been found.[9] India's printed textiles have probably influenced fabric design and manufacture more than the textiles from any other country. Block printing, wax resist printing, painting, and tie-dying were all used in India.[10] In block printing, a block of wood or other material is carved with the design. Then the block is inked and pressed onto the fabric. In wax resist (batik), sections of the fabric that are not to be dyed are covered with wax. In tie-dying, the fabric is tied in knots and then submerged in the dye. Wax resist printing came to Java from India at the start of the fifth century A.D. and developed into batik.[11]

---

[8]Meda Parker Johnson and Glen Kaufman, *Design on Fabric* (New York: Van Nostrand Reinhold Co., 1967), p. 9.
[9]Ibid., p. 10.
[10]Ibid., pp. 10-12.
[11]Ibid., p. 14.

Figure 6-6. Vertical Alternate Repeat in a Diamond Layout.

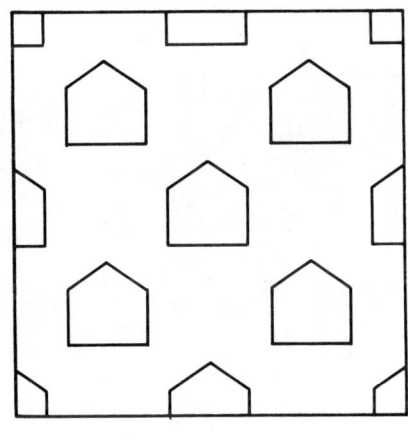

Diamond

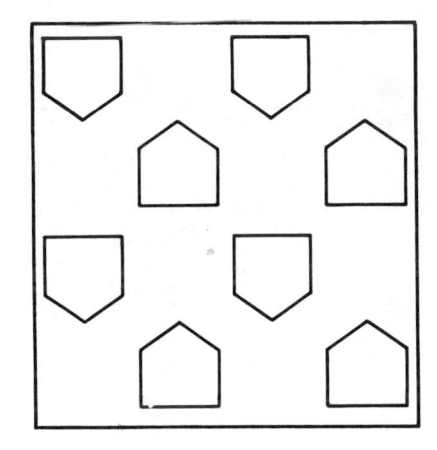

Diamond/Vertical Alternate

Figure 6-7. "Mary's Needlepoint" Design by Fieldcrest Combines Geometric Shapes, Flowers, Violins, and Hearts.

Fabric Design

The Chinese began block printing about 400 B.C. and by the eighth century A.D. were greatly influencing the Japanese.[12] The Japanese used stamps, stencils, wax resists, and painting.

Fabrics were being block printed in Europe by the tenth century, but no craft guilds for textile printers existed during the Middle Ages.[13] By the seventeenth century, Indian and East Indian fabrics were being imported by Europeans. The designs were copied by the Europeans. An Englishman, William Sherwin, began printing calico in 1676.[14] In about 1750 the Irishman Francis Nixon introduced the copperplate method of printing.[15] In copperplate printing a copper cylindrical plate is cut with the lines of the design. The plate is inked, wiped clean, and rolled onto the fabric. The ink in the cuts of the plate transfers to the fabric. In the 1770's the English began roller printing, a process differing from copperplate printing in that a hard rubber roller is used. Christophe-Philippe Oberkampf used copperplates in the French print works of Jouy founded in 1759.[16] John Heuson, an American, printed calico in Philadelphia in 1770, but America did not make significant strides in fabric printing until the twentieth century.[17]

---

[12]Ibid., pp. 12-13.
[13]Stuart Robinson, *A History of Printed Textiles* (Cambridge, Mass.: The M.I.T. Press, 1970), p. 11.
[14]Ibid., p. 15.
[15]Johnson and Kaufman, *Design on Fabric,* p. 16.
[16]Ibid., p. 18.
[17]Ibid., p. 24.

Projects for Fabric Design

1. Create a simple design motif suitable for fabric. Use the design for the following repeats:
   A. Block
   B. Half drop
   C. Diamond
   D. Alternating
2. Design a more elaborate repeating motif. Render it in three different color schemes. (See Types of Color Schemes inside front cover.)
3. Print your own simple repeating design using some of the following:
   A. Carved potato
   B. Sponge
   C. Potato masher
   D. Cut cork
   E. Brushes
   F. Linoleum block
   G. Other common objects
4. Research the history of textile printing in one of the geographical areas listed below and write a report.
   A. India
   B. The Orient
   C. Africa
   D. Central and South America
   E. The Middle East
   F. Europe
   G. United States

Bibliography

Alexander, Mary Jean. ***Handbook of Decorative Design and Ornament.*** New York: L. Amiêl Publishing Co., 1965.

Bates, Kenneth F. ***Basic Design: Principles and Practice.*** New York: Funk & Wagnalls, 1975.

Bevlin, Marjorie Elliott. ***Design Through Discovery.*** 3rd ed. New York: Holt, Rinehart & Winston, Inc., 1977.

Johnson, Meda Parker, and Kaufman, Glen. ***Design on Fabric.*** New York: Van Nostrand Reinhold Co., 1967.

Proud, Nora. ***Textile Printing and Dyeing Simplified.*** New York: Arco Publishing Co., Inc., 1974.

Robinson, Stuart. ***A History of Printed Textiles.*** Cambridge, Mass.: The M.I.T. Press, 1970.

7

Fashion Drawing

Many jobs in the fashion world require sketching ability. It is true that a buyer, coordinator, or stylist is neither a designer nor an illustrator, however, the person who can translate fashion experiences into sketches of garments or accessories will more capably fill these positions. A written description is never as clear as a sketch. A designer or an illustrator usually spends many years studying anatomy and drawing technique in order to render fashion designs of the exceptional quality seen today. Since your sketches most likely will be used as a memory jog to write reports from, or as thumbnail sketches to accompany reports, they should be simple and clear. In sketching it will be helpful to perfect some basic figure poses that can be adapted to whatever fashions you see.

Basic Figure Drawing

Everyone can learn to draw a basic fashion figure. First the proportions of anatomy must be understood. The average person stands 7½ heads high. This means that the distance from the top of the head to the tips of the toes is 7½ times the length of the head. Look at Figure 7-1 View A, a skeletal outline of the female figure. Now look at yourself and try to find a shape that would best represent all of your body parts—it is an elongated oval—a large one forms the trunk, narrow ones form the legs, arms, hands, feet, and neck, and a rounder one forms the head. See Figure 7-1 View B. View C is the realistic outline of a female figure and follows easily once the ovals are drawn. To draw a realistic figure, think of connecting the ovals with a flowing line, yet adjusting the line to the skeleton, which adds these changes: breadth to the shoulders, space between upper arms and trunk, a waistline, a rounded hip line, and narrowed lower thighs and calves.

Study a female figure. Does it conform to the 7½-head average figure, which places the bust at 2 heads, the waist at 3, the knees at 5½, and the ankles at 7? Using ovals, draw the figure that you just observed. Then draw the realistic outline.

For fashion drawing, an 8½-head figure is generally used. This figure is called a "croquis" (KRO-ke). See Figures 7-2 and 7-3 for the proportions of the female and male croquis. In a magazine or newspaper the fashion figure is often exaggerated beyond 8½ heads to 9½ or 10½ heads, since the emphasis is on the line of the clothing rather than on perfect proportion.

An important principle to understand before beginning to draw is that every figure

128　　　　　　　　　　　　　　　　　　　　　　　　　　　　**Fashion: Color, Line, and Design**

Figure 7-1. Three Steps in Drawing a 7½-Head Basic Fashion Figure.

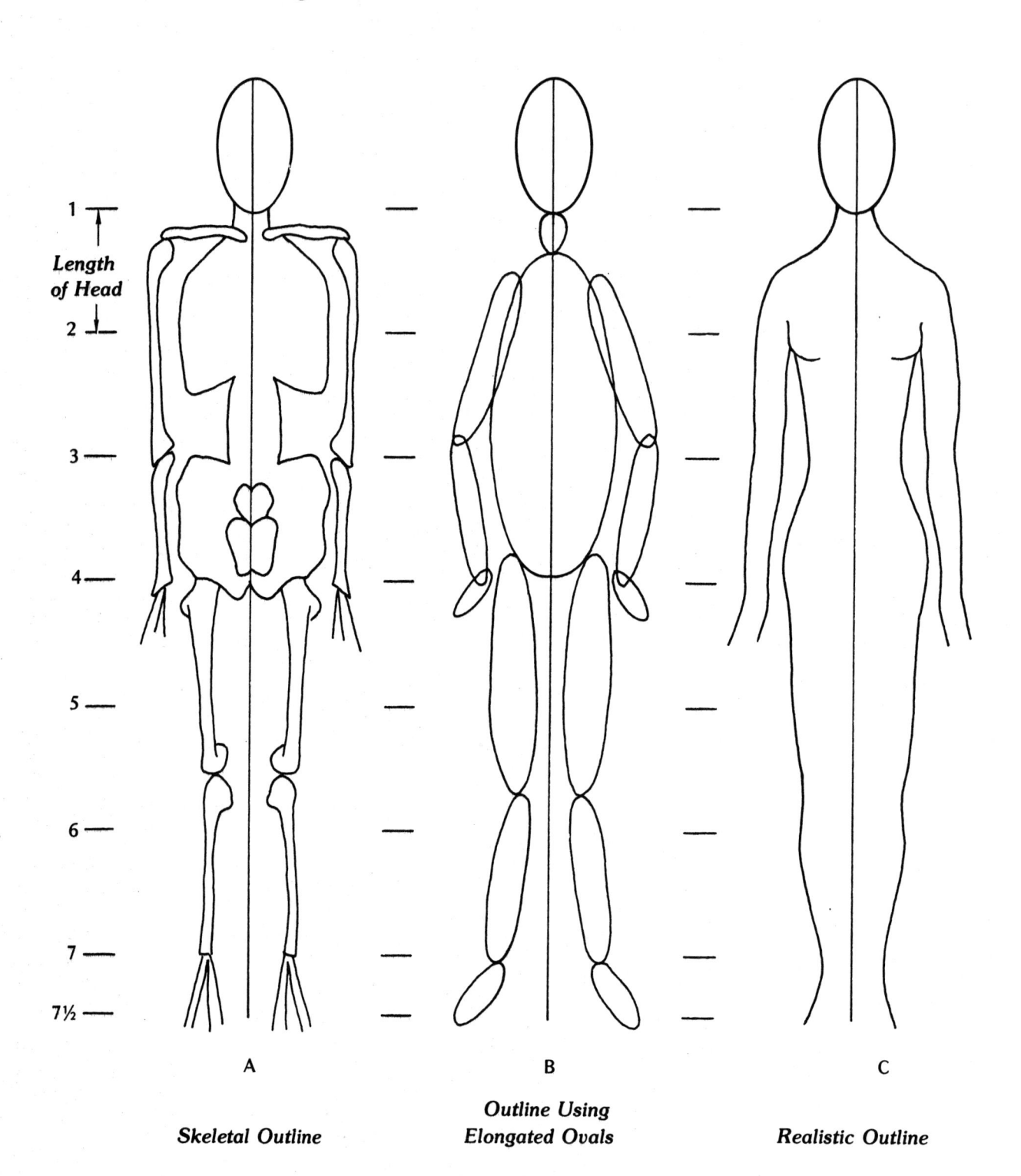

A

Skeletal Outline

B

Outline Using Elongated Ovals

C

Realistic Outline

Fashion Drawing

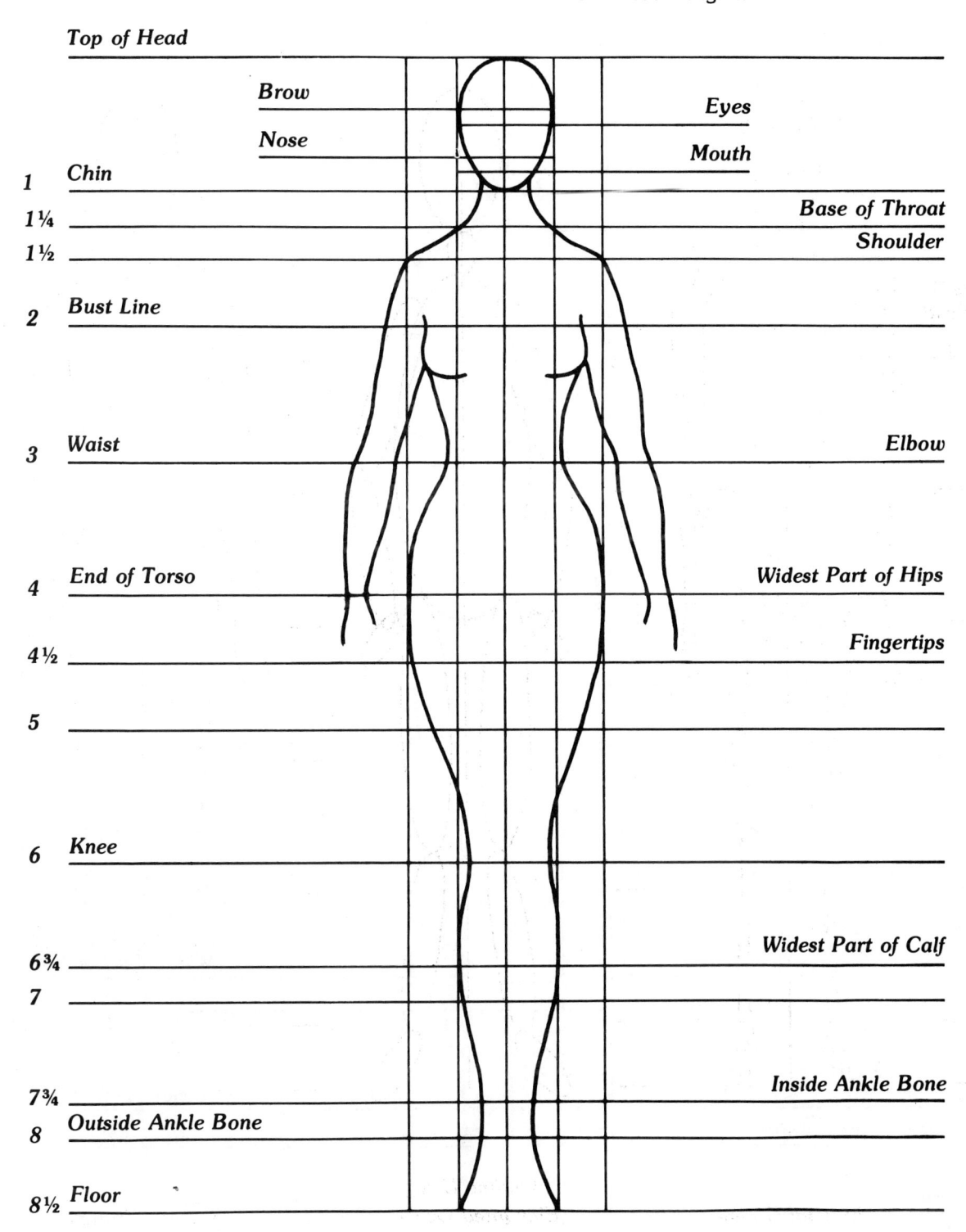

Figure 7-2. Female Croquis, Extended to 8½ Head Lengths.

	Top of Head	
	Brow	Eyes
	Nose	Mouth
1	Chin	
1¼		Base of Throat
1½		Shoulder
2	Bust Line	
3	Waist	Elbow
4	End of Torso	Widest Part of Hips
4½		Fingertips
5		
6	Knee	
6¾		Widest Part of Calf
7		
7¾		Inside Ankle Bone
8	Outside Ankle Bone	
8½	Floor	

130　　　　　　　　　　　　　　　　　　　　　　　　　　　　　　　　　Fashion: Color, Line, and Design

Figure 7-3. Male Croquis, Extended to 8½ Head Lengths.

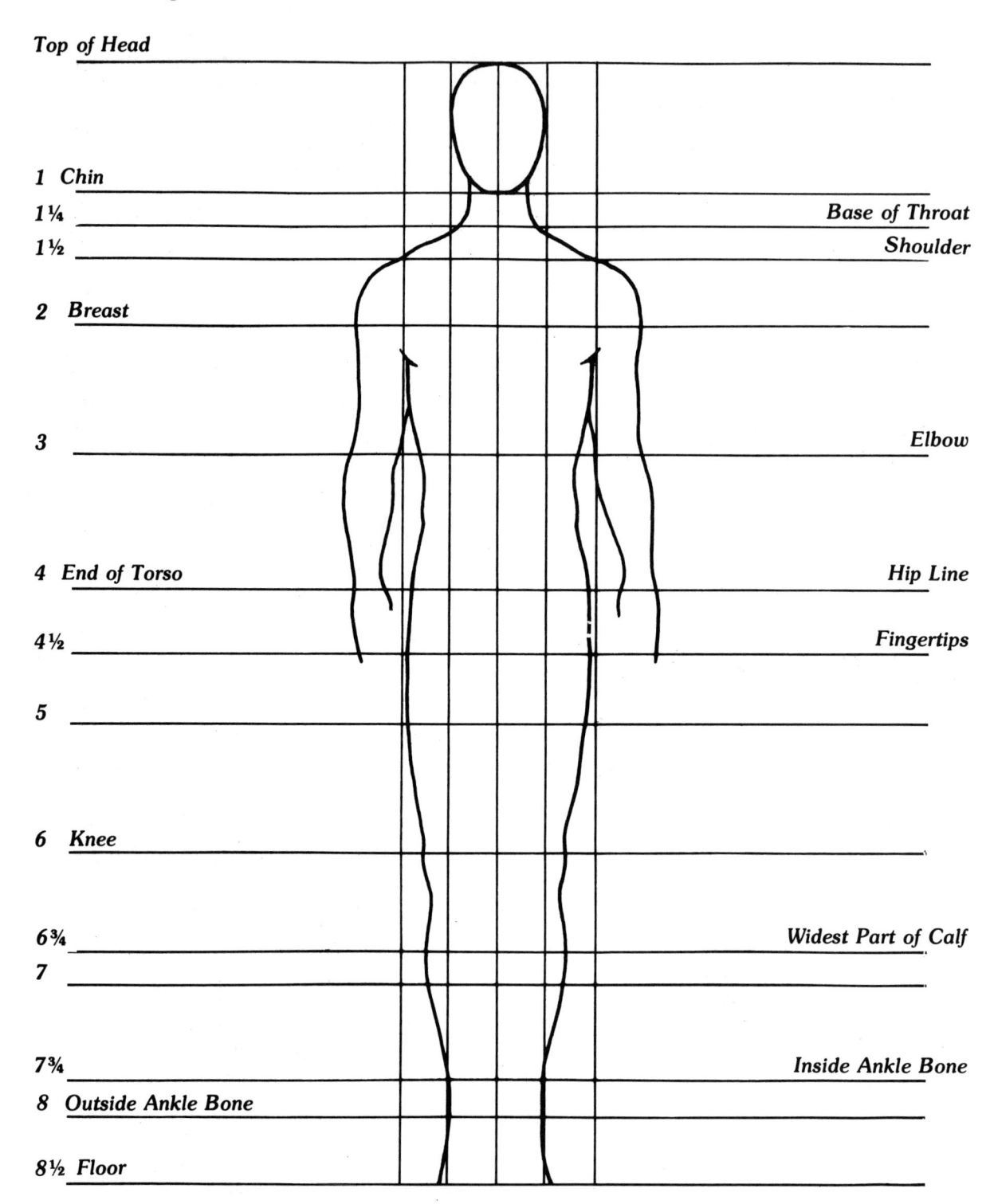

Top of Head

1　Chin
1¼　　　　　　　　　　　　　　　　　　　　　　　　　　　　　　　　　*Base of Throat*
1½　　　　　　　　　　　　　　　　　　　　　　　　　　　　　　　　　*Shoulder*

2　Breast

3　　　　　　　　　　　　　　　　　　　　　　　　　　　　　　　　　　*Elbow*

4　End of Torso　　　　　　　　　　　　　　　　　　　　　　　　　　　*Hip Line*
4½　　　　　　　　　　　　　　　　　　　　　　　　　　　　　　　　　*Fingertips*

5

6　Knee

6¾　　　　　　　　　　　　　　　　　　　　　　　　　　　　　　　　　*Widest Part of Calf*
7

7¾　　　　　　　　　　　　　　　　　　　　　　　　　　　　　　　　　*Inside Ankle Bone*
8　Outside Ankle Bone

8½　Floor

Fashion Drawing

must be balanced. The balance line is a straight line running from the pit of the neck through the body down to the foot supporting the weight (see Figure 7-4 View A). If the weight is equally distributed on both feet, then the balance line will center between them, as shown in Figure 7-4 View B. Three-quarters, side, and back views are often more suitable than full-front views. Look through fashion magazines for recurring poses.

Clothing is designed for the body in movement, and therefore action sketches are more realistic than still ones. Body action is indicated by changing the height of the shoulders or hips (see Figure 7-4 Views C, D, and E). Arm and leg positions also indicate movement, as shown in Figure 7-4 Views C and D. Do not exaggerate the positions, however, or the emphasis switches from the clothes, where it belongs, to the figure.

A combination stick and oval figure makes a good starting point for simple fashion drawing. The first figure you will draw is full-front with the weight on the left foot and hands on hips. Draw the 8½-head grid for initial drawings to make sure the proportions are correct, then follow these steps:

Step 1. Draw the head, balance line, shoulder line, and hip line, as shown in Figure 7-5.

Step 2. Draw the arm and leg lines.

Step 3. Add ovals for body shape.

Step 4. Round out the body silhouette by connecting and trimming the ovals. Figure 7-6 shows the same process with a three-quarters pose. Figures 7-7 and 7-8 show a variety of poses. Practice these steps until you can draw a realistic figure in several poses, visualizing the ovals instead of drawing them first.

Drawing Clothing

Once you understand figure proportions and have mastered some basic fashion poses it is time to go on to sketching clothing. Keep the figure simple with as few lines as necessary. The apparel details are important and should be accurate. The sketch should show the movement of the clothing on the body.

In your sketch the body should look three dimensional and the clothing should curve around it. Avoid making a sketch that looks like a flat paper doll. Where the clothing touches the body there will be folds caused by the action of the body (see Figure 7-9 View A). There will be folds formed by the flow of the fabric (View B). There will be folds formed by the design of the garment—pleats or gathers for example (View C). Many times a sketch will have all three types of folds (View D).

Pose and Clothing Relationship

The figure pose and the garment style should be in harmony with each other. Active sportswear will look better on a figure showing movement, and a couture evening design will look better on an inactive figure. Constantly studying fashion magazines and newspaper fashion ads will keep you abreast of popular poses and of illustration styles. Fashion illustration styles change just as fashions do. The illustrative figures are exaggerated. The proportions may change with the style of the clothing, since the emphasis is not on total accuracy of detail but on eye appeal. Establish a portfolio of figures to work with. You might choose to carry it with you most of the time, or carry predrawn figures inside a book. Then when you need a sketch you can impose the clothing over the predrawn figures.

When you do a sketch, it is not necessary to do an accurate rendering of the fabrication. Written notes can describe the type and color of the fabric. You might be able to get a swatch to pin to the sketch. If a swatch is not

132   Fashion: Color, Line, and Design

Figure 7-4. The Balance Line Runs from the Neck through the Body to the Foot.

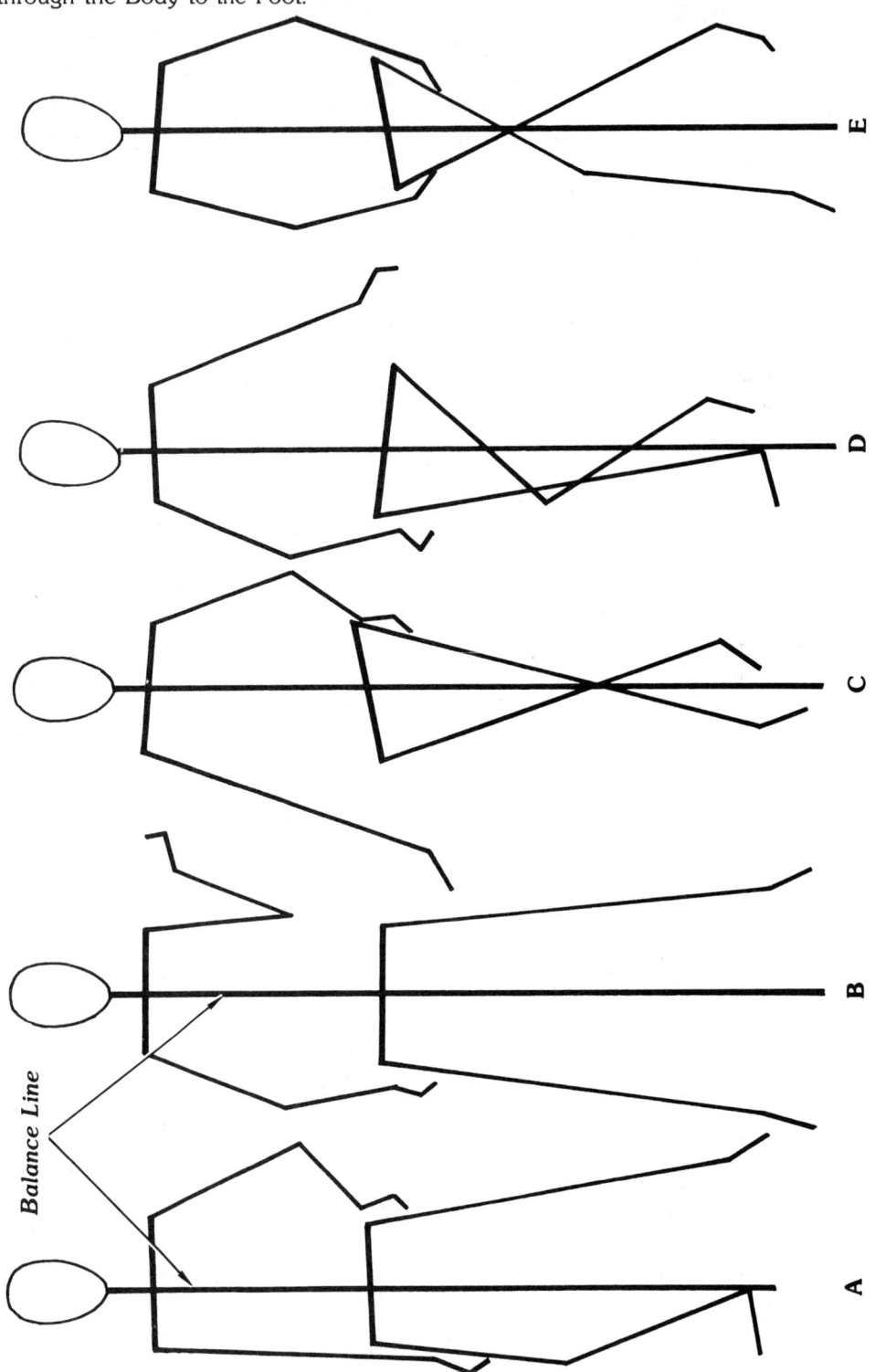

Fashion Drawing

Figure 7-5. Steps in Drawing a Full-Front Fashion Figure.

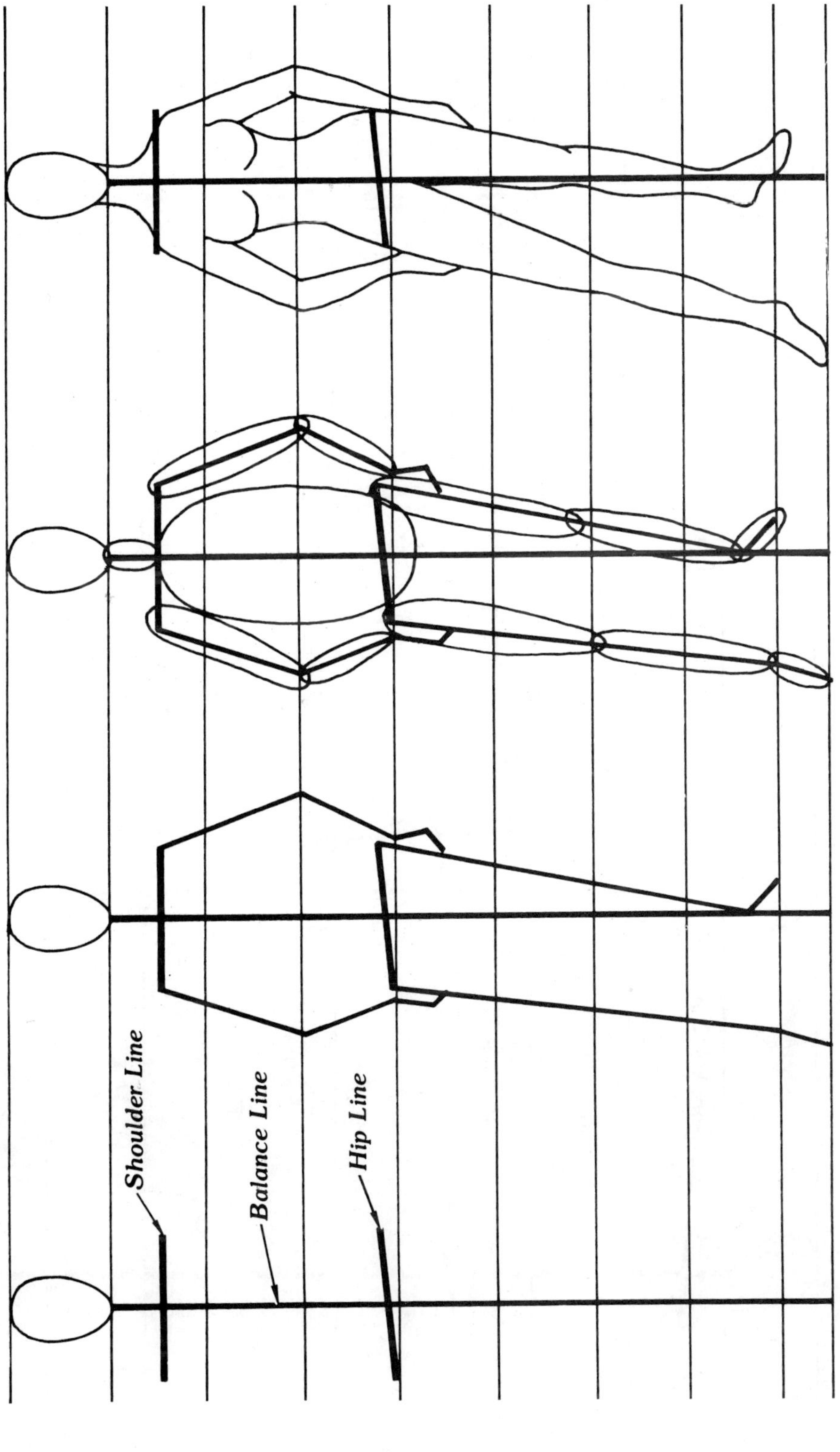

134   **Fashion: Color, Line, and Design**

Figure 7-6. Steps in Drawing a Three-Quarters Pose Fashion Figure.

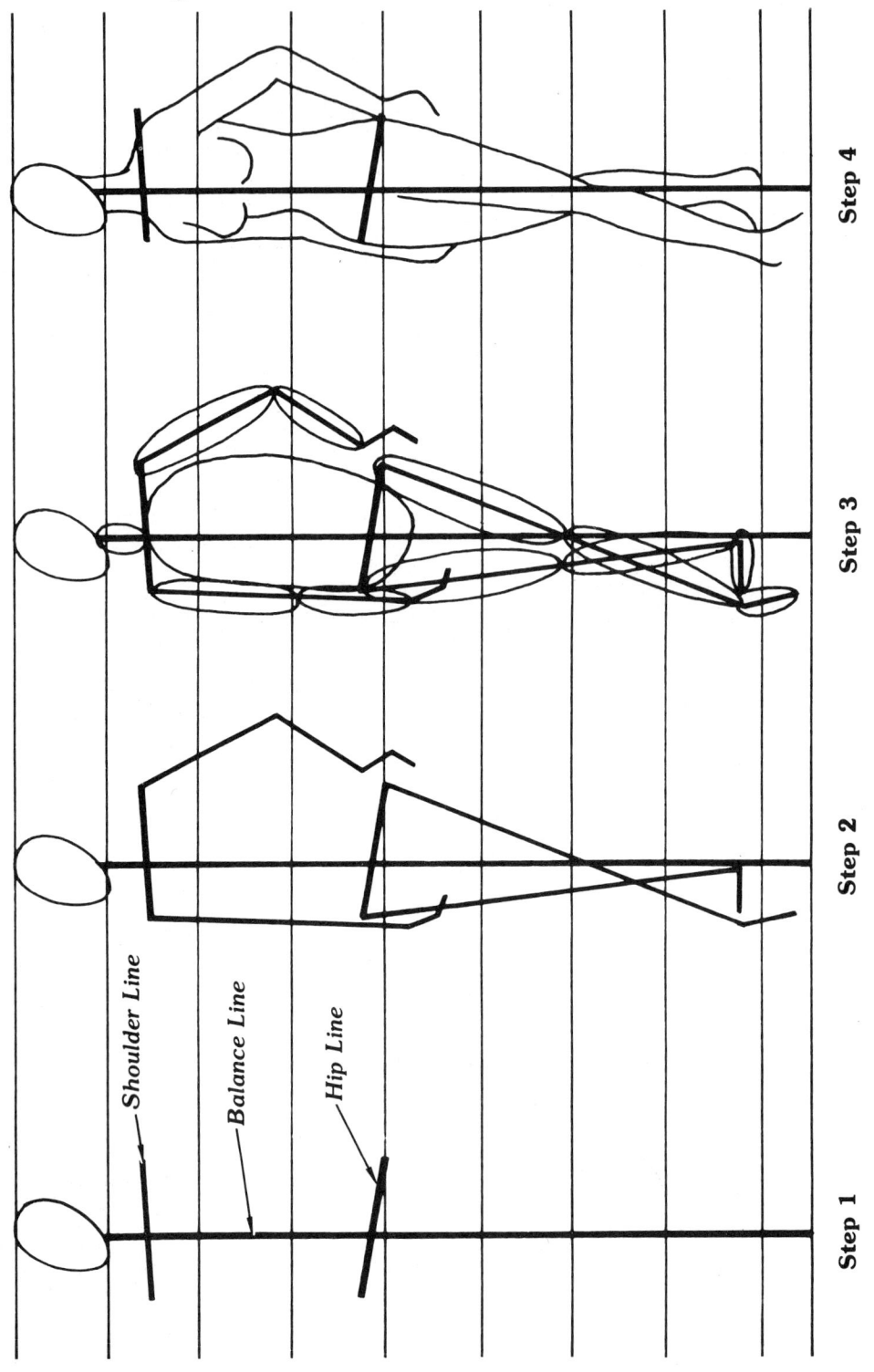

Fashion Drawing 135

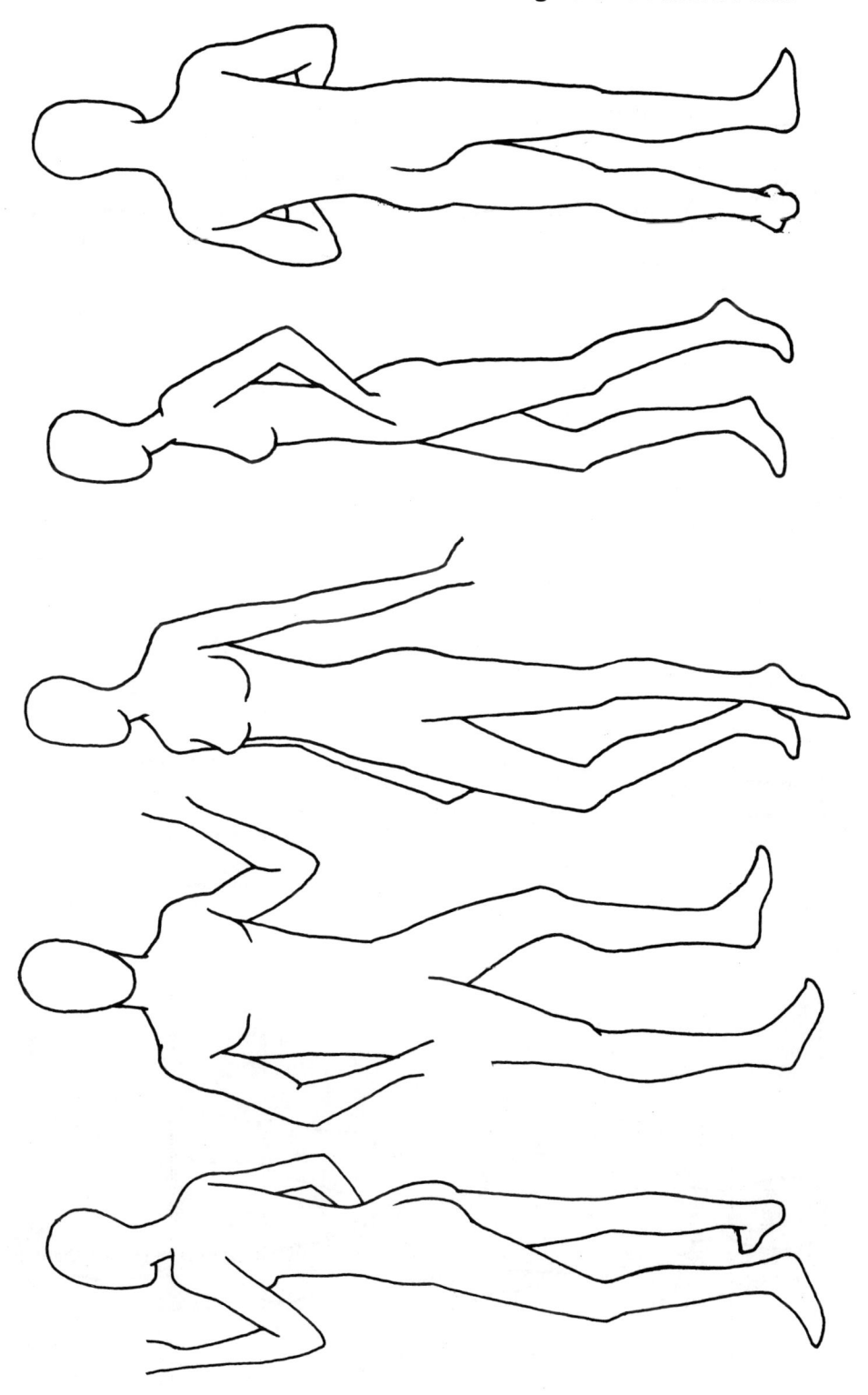

Figure 7-7. Fashion Poses.

136   Fashion: Color, Line, and Design

Figure 7-8. Fashion Poses.

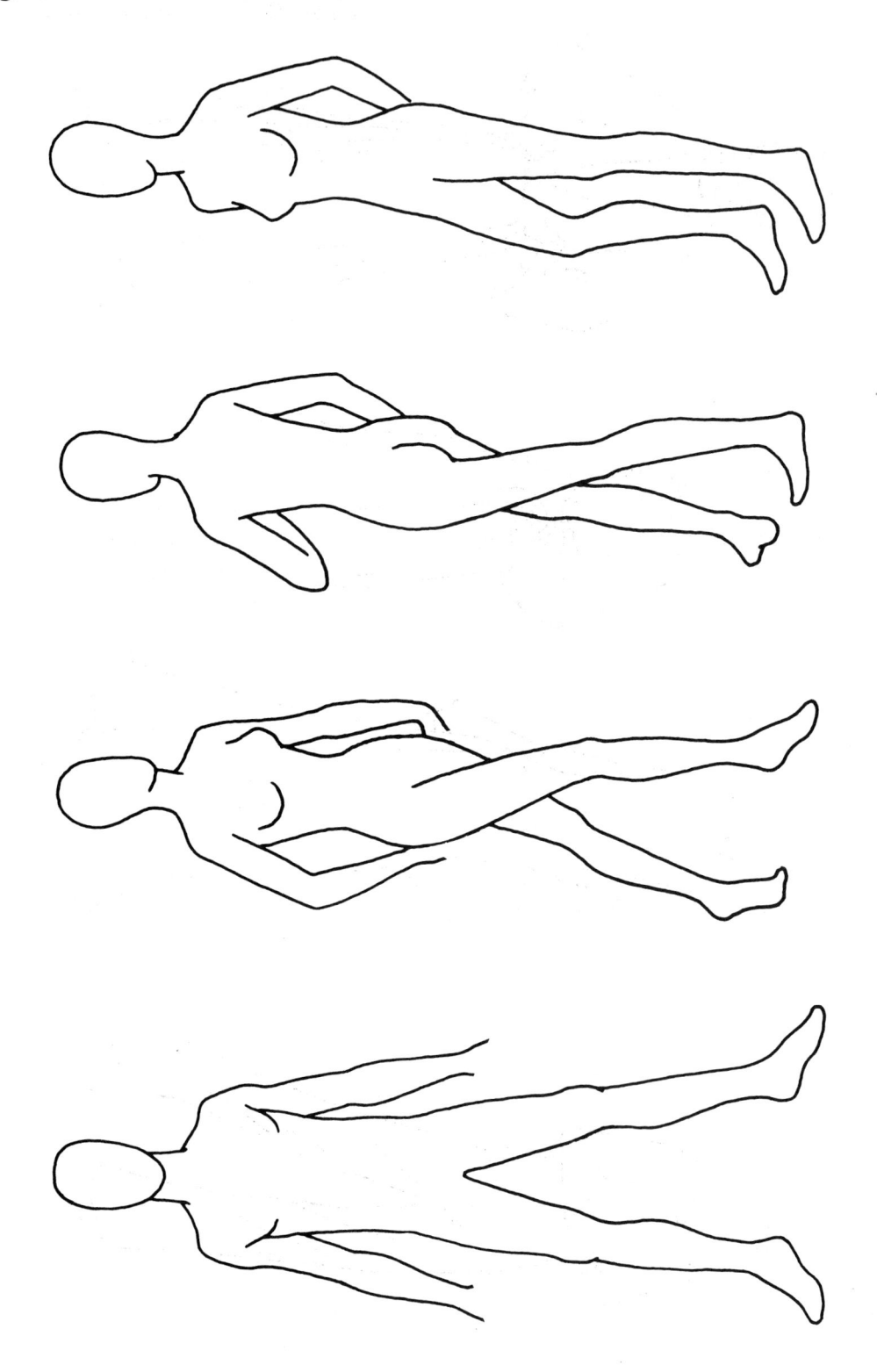

Fashion Drawing 137

Figure 7-9. Show the Movement of Clothing on the Body in Fashion Sketches.

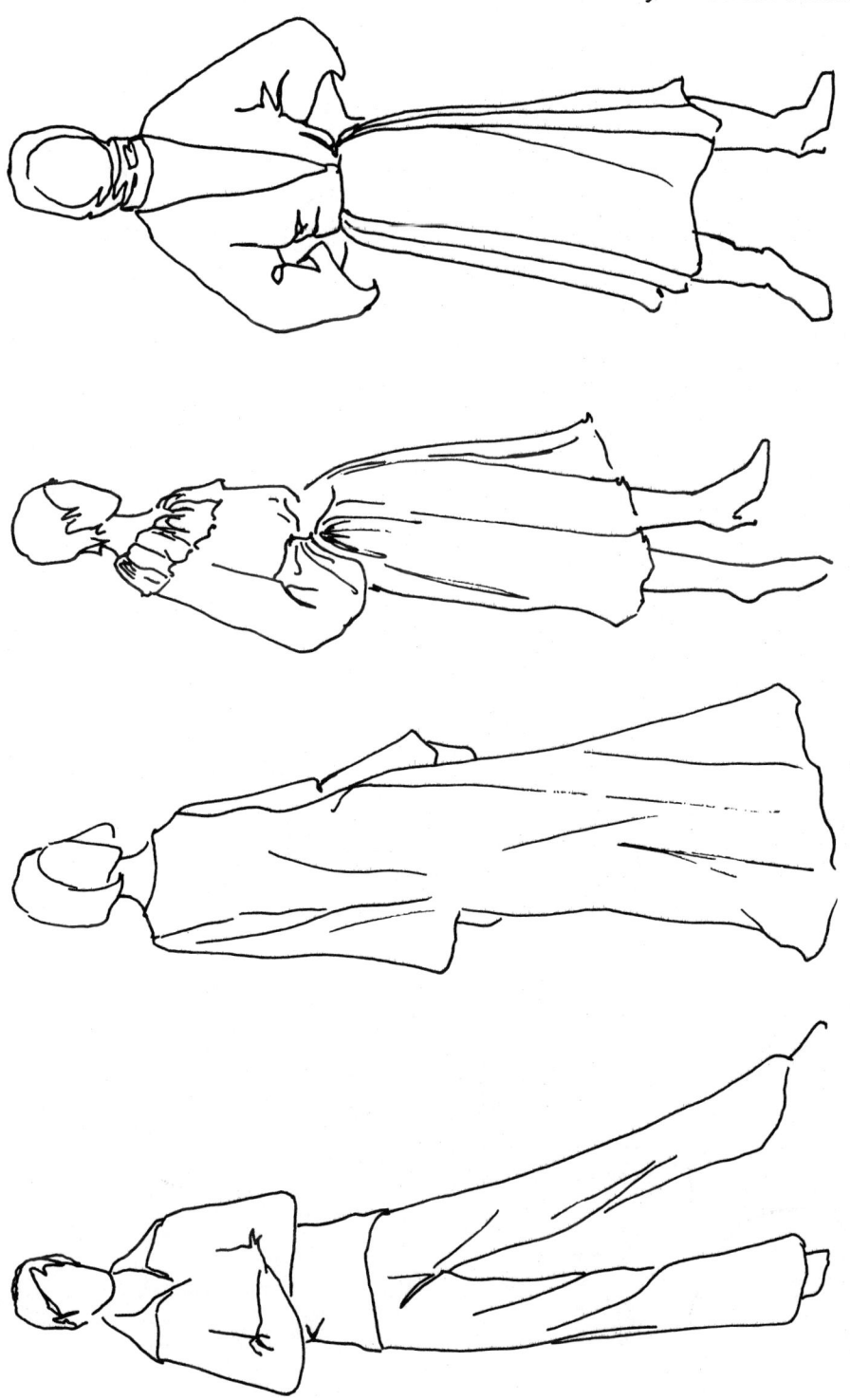

available and a description does not do justice to a print, you should be able to do a simple drawing of it.

Pose and Customer Size/Image Relationship

The figure type and pose used in drawing should reflect the intended customer. The potential customer wants a certain "look" that is the result of several factors including age and body shape and size. Today sophistication and style influence the look of the potential customer. Age is always a factor, but the fashion image comes first. The *misses* size customer is a well-proportioned female of average height. The *petite misses* size customer is shorter. The junior size customer is well proportioned but shorter waisted and not quite as tall. There is a combined *misses/junior* size today. The woman's size figure is larger, average in height, and mature. The *half size* figure is short, full, and has a short back waist length. An age range has been associated with each figure type. Juniors are generally depicted in their teens or early twenties, misses are depicted in their thirties, and half size and women's sizes are depicted out of their thirties and older.

At some time in your career you might want to take a fashion drawing course. Certainly it will be beneficial. But until you do so the techniques you have learned here should enable you to view and reproduce fashion lines intelligently. Your knowledge of color, silhouette, and design motifs, combined with basic fashion drawing, should enable you to take accurate notes and write well-prepared reports.

Projects for Fashion Drawing

1. Go through a fashion magazine or newspaper ads and find 10 different poses. With tracing paper overlays, put in the balance line, shoulder line, and hip line.
2. Using the tracing paper overlays from the previous assignment, draw the stick and oval figures. On another sheet of tracing paper, contour each rough figure into a fashion figure.
3. Make a portfolio of 20 different fashion poses.
4. Find 10 fashion photographs showing the entire figure. Do a fashion sketch of each.
5. Collect 10 fashion illustrations from magazines and newspapers. Overlay them with tracing paper and measure the proportions. Discuss the results.
6. Using geometric forms and lines, design an outfit suitable for each of the following figure types. Complete each design in color.
   A. Tall figure
   B. Short figure
   C. Slender figure
   D. Stout figure
   E. Pear-shaped figure
   F. T-shaped figure

Bibliography

Dilley, Romilda. ***Drawing Women's Fashions.*** New York: Watson-Guptill Publications, 1959.

Ireland, Patrick John. ***Fashion Design Drawing.*** New York: Halsted Press, 1975.

Ireland, Patrick John. ***Fashion Drawing for Advertising.*** New York: John Wiley & Sons, 1974.

Peck, Stephen Rogers. ***Atlas of Human Anatomy for the Artist.*** New York: Oxford University Press, 1951.

Sheppard, Joseph. ***Drawing the Male Figure.*** Cincinnati, Ohio: Watson-Guptill, 1976.